BETTER
BACKGAMMON

Also by Tim Holland:

Beginning Backgammon

*Backgammon for People Who
   Hate to Lose*

BETTER
BACKGAMMON

TIM HOLLAND

David McKay Company, Inc.
New York

BETTER BACKGAMMON
COPYRIGHT © 1974 BY Tim Holland

First Tartan paperback edition, 1979

And again to Lona

*Illustrations and Design by
Remo R. Duchi*

LIBRARY OF CONGRESS CATALOG CARD NUMBER: 74-82267

ISBN: 0-679-14126-X

1 2 3 4 5 6 7 8 9 10

MANUFACTURED IN THE UNITED STATES OF AMERICA

INTRODUCTION

TIM HOLLAND NEEDS LITTLE INTRODUCTION—but perhaps this book does.

Mr. Holland's name is almost synonymous with the game of backgammon, though the game is considerably older. Winner for three consecutive times of the World's Championship of Backgammon and twice the winner of the International Championship of Backgammon, Tim Holland is an accredited backgammon master. Few, if any, are his equal at the game.

Any publisher would be proud to have Tim Holland as one of its authors; this publisher is doubly proud, for *Better Backgammon* is his second book for David McKay.

Better Backgammon is a logical sequel to Mr. Holland's first book,

Beginning Backgammon. But this book isn't a *Son of Beginning Backgammon*, although the two volumes bear a family resemblance. Each is a practical learning tool, through which the reader *learns by playing* against the master, Tim Holland. *Better Backgammon* picks up where *Beginning Backgammon* left off. Mr. Holland is a marvelous teacher; he understands that a novice must enjoy a game to learn it well, and he has incorporated this principle into each of his two books.

Beginning Backgammon started the beginner down the right road to backgammon mastery by pitting the reader against the author in five games. *Better Backgammon* is a book of problems—common, yet perplexing, situations that a player is likely to encounter in one or another future games. Like *Beginning Backgammon*, Mr. Holland's knotty problems are illustrated with easy-to-follow diagrams.

You, the reader, have an interest in backgammon, or you wouldn't be reading this page. Perhaps you know that it is the oldest game in recorded history—an ancient game that is perfectly suited to modern times, an "aristrocrat of games" that has popular and growing appeal.

Ancient Greeks played it, Persians played it, Egyptians played it, and it is said that Emperor Claudius not only played it but wrote a book about it. Roman centurions carried backgammon to England, where the game was known as "tables" until well into the seventeenth century. For years only English knights and the nobility were allowed to play it. The word "backgammon," or "back game," from the Middle English *gamen*, came into vogue sometime later. The English also refined the rules into an approximation of today's game—except for the use of the doubling cube, which was introduced in the mid-1920s.

The popularization of backgammon in recent years excites Mr. Holland, who is pleased with the game's high-born heritage but is even more pleased to encounter a host of new backgammon fans outside the hallowed gaming rooms of exclusive clubs.

Before you take the plunge and face up to Mr. Holland's Problem 1, a few more words about the author might be appropriate. Tim Holland has been called "the Babe Ruth of Backgammon" by a major newspaper and "backgammon's James Bond" by a national magazine. He is comfortable with both descriptions, as comfortable as he is with the major titles he has won at the board. It is difficult to imagine Tim Holland *un*comfortable any place—in his publishers' office, in public, or in a gaming room. Mr. Holland's goal—"mission," if you will—is to make you more comfortable and confident when you are playing his favorite game. *Better Backgammon* should show you the way.

—THE PUBLISHERS

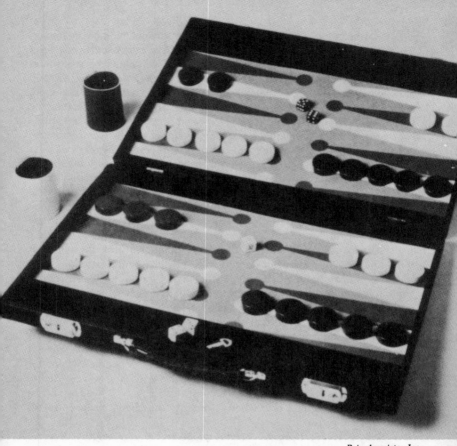

FROM THE MOMENT I first laid eyes on a backgammon board, I have found the game to be irresistibly fascinating—whether playing it, watching, or merely lending a consoling ear to the "you-wouldn't-believe-what-happened-to-me!" stories. (It seems that all backgammon devotees, whatever their level of expertise, are convinced that occult forces are at work to make their lives miserable.) Among the many rewards I've gained as a result of this fascination, perhaps the most pleasurable has involved making it possible for others to enjoy this magnificently beautiful game.

1

Contrary to what some may believe, my proficiency at backgammon has not been achieved through some innate ability; my expertise is not a "gift." Rather, it has resulted from thousands of hours of study and experimentation. I am convinced that with backgammon—as with all endeavors that require specialized learning—the deeper and more comprehensive the practitioner's knowledge, the more gratification he will derive from it. I am also convinced that there are but three prerequisites to an individual's reaching a level of excellence at games in general: (1) the desire, (2) the time, and (3) competent instruction.

In my case, fortunately, prerequisite number one was immediately fulfilled, for within five minutes of watching my first backgammon game, I had become unequivocally addicted to the pursuit of its intricacies. This addiction, nurtured at the time by my supreme egotism, supplied all the "desire" I needed. (In retrospect I realize that this "supreme egotism"—as undesirable a personality trait as it usually is—was totally necessary to me during the many hours I spent learning the game. It would have been difficult to find a more compelling motivation.)

Prerequisite number two was rather easily met, for I had plenty of time. But number three—the need for competent instruction—presented a problem. Although most of the people I was playing with had been accepting doubles for several decades, I began to suspect that their movement of the men and their use of the doubling block left much to be desired. It wasn't long before my suspicions regarding the competence of my "mentors" were confirmed, for on countless occasions when, for example, I would ask my partners in a chouette why they had refused to let me make a certain play, they could answer only, "Well—it's just wrong." The same held true when it came to the giving or accepting of doubles.

Now, if you've been wondering where this rather lengthy dissertation is leading, the answer is this: Our common goal in this book is to fulfill prerequisite number three for you. The first two prerequisites, of course, depend on *you*.

At this point in your backgammon career you should already know all of the rules, the opening moves, and the terms. The only information contained in this book other than the problems themselves are (1) a chart on entering men from the bar and (2) the following short explanation of the laws of probability:

There are 36 possible combinations of rolls on the dice in backgammon. This figure is arrived at by multiplying the 6 numbers on one die by the 6 numbers on the second die. The following chart lists these possible combinations.

Double 1	1
Double 2	1
Double 3	1
Double 4	1
Double 5	1
Double 6	1
1 and 2, or 2 and 1	2
1 and 3, or 3 and 1	2
1 and 4, or 4 and 1	2
1 and 5, or 5 and 1	2
1 and 6, or 6 and 1	2
2 and 3, or 3 and 2	2
2 and 4, or 4 and 2	2
2 and 5, or 5 and 2	2
2 and 6, or 6 and 2	2
3 and 4, or 4 and 3	2
3 and 5, or 5 and 3	2
3 and 6, or 6 and 3	2
4 and 5, or 5 and 4	2
4 and 6, or 6 and 4	2
5 and 6, or 6 and 5	2
TOTAL	36

If you examine this chart you will see that fifteen combinations occur twice. For example, let's assume that one die is red and the second die is green. The combination 1 and 6 occurs when the green die has a 1 and the red die shows 6, and also when the red die shows a 1 and green die shows a 6. The same is true of all other combinations. The fifteen combinations that occur twice account for 30 of the 36 possible combinations—the remaining 6 are doubles, which occur only once each. Therefore, a specific combination such as 6 and 1 should occur, on the average, twice in every 36 rolls. This will hold true for any other specific combination, with the exception of doubles. A specific double has a probability of occurring only one time out of 36.

Simple, isn't it!

And, strangely enough, the above laws of probability may be the key to *Better Backgammon* for you.

It's time to play—and learn. So let's begin.

PROBLEM 1

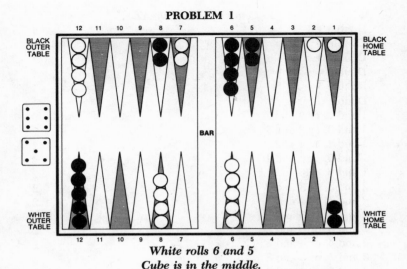

White rolls 6 and 5
Cube is in the middle.

The correct play is to make Black's bar point. This establishes a good defensive position. It will also enable you to play a running game if you roll double 2s, 3s, 4s, or 5s, which will allow you to move in safety toward your home board. It would be incorrect to move your blot on Black's 1 point to safety on Black's 12 point. Your remaining blot on Black's 2 point is now in danger of being cut off from escape or of being pointed on.

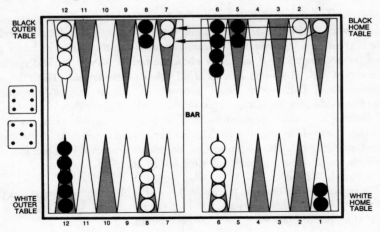

4

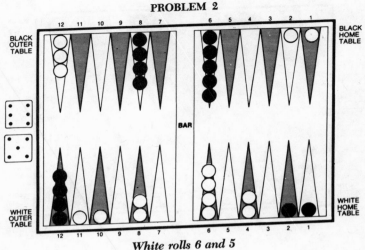

White rolls 6 and 5
Cube is in the middle.

The correct play is to make White's 5 point. The tremendous value of having your 5 point at this juncture of the game far outweighs any other move.

You are putting pressure on Black's blots in your home board in two ways: first, with the start of a formidable blockade which restricts Black's forward movement and escape, and, second, with the threat of making additional points in your board which could put Black on the rim.

Since there is no threat to your men in Black's home board at this moment, you should not consider either the play of making Black's bar point or the move of one man from Black's 1 point to Black's 12 point.

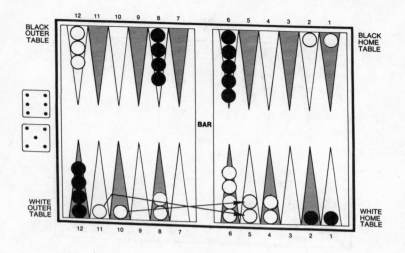

●　●　●

PROBLEM 3

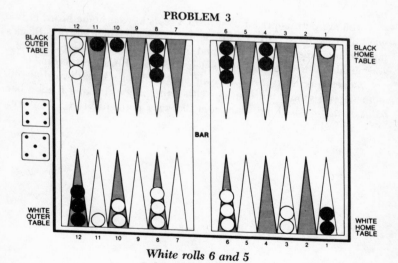

White rolls 6 and 5
Cube is in the middle.

6

The correct play is to move one man from Black's 1 point to Black's 12 point. Black is threatening to shut off your escape route. This may be the last time you will be able to get out of his trap; since the opportunity has presented itself, you must take advantage of it. Another reason for selecting this move in preference to that of making your 5 point is that if Black does not hit your blot on your 11 point (17 to 1 against your being hit) or make your 5 point (only double 4s), you will have several combinations available to you on your next roll that will make either your 5 point, 4 point, or bar point.

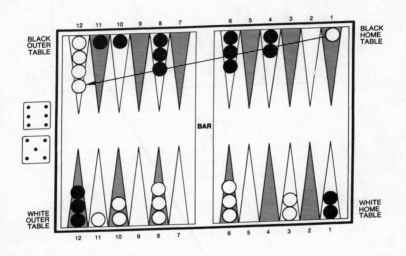

PROBLEM 4

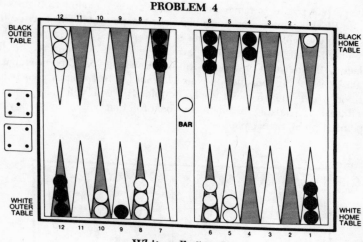

White rolls 5 and 4
Cube is in the middle.

The correct play is to make Black's 5 point. By having this point, you prevent Black from blocking your escape. You also have a landing spot in the event you are hit sometime later in the game.

You hope on your next roll to make your bar point, 4, or 3 point, which would end, more or less, Black's attempts to escape with his men on your 1 point.

The alternative move is tempting but incorrect. It is to enter on Black's 5 point and hit Black's blot on your 9 point. This would give Black a fourth man in your home board, perhaps allowing him to make a second point there, which could prove embarrassing to you later on.

8

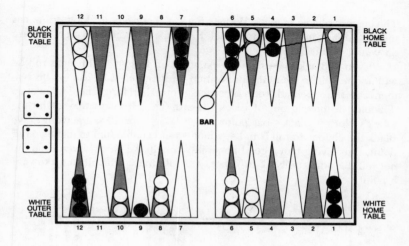

PROBLEM 5

White rolls 6 and 1
Black owns the cube.

The correct play is to make White's 5 point. Your 5 point long prime has made it almost impossible for Black to escape with his two men that are on your 1 point.

Even if Black makes his bar point, 5, or 4 on his next roll he will not be able to maintain his position for long unless he can get his two men out from behind your blockade. You, therefore, should have no difficulty in moving out of Black's board. The alternate play of hitting Black's blot on Black's bar point and making your 10 point would give Black the chance to roll 5 and 4, which would enable him to make your 5 point, thus giving him a good possibility to win the game. Even if he did not roll this admittedly 17 to 1 shot, you will find it difficult to make your 5 point.

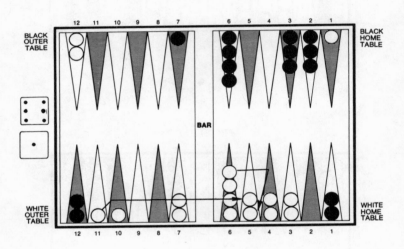

● ● ●

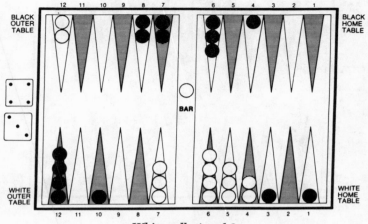

White rolls 4 and 3
Black owns the cube.

The correct play is to enter on Black's 4 point, hitting Black's blot, move one man 3 from White's 6 point to White's 3 point, hitting Black's blot. What may seem to be an unnecessary exposure of a blot on your 3 point is an attempt by you to prevent Black from establishing this point. If your blot is not hit (Black has 13 chances out of 36—any 3, double 1s, or double 2s), in all probability you will be able to establish this point yourself, thus creating a 5 long block and making Black's position untenable.

An alternate use of your 3 to hit Black's blot on your 10 point is incorrect for two reasons. One is that this move would give Black 13 chances to establish your 3 point (any 3, double 2s, or 1s). With the correct play Black has only 1 chance to make your 3 point (double 3s). The second reason is that you have given Black a fourth man back. If he is fortunate, he will be able to make 2 points in your board, thus creating an effective position that will enable him to play a back game.

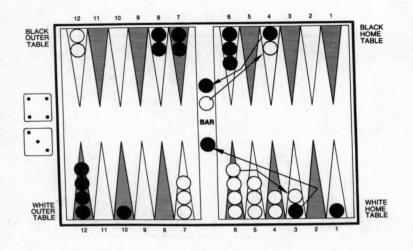

• • •

PROBLEM 7

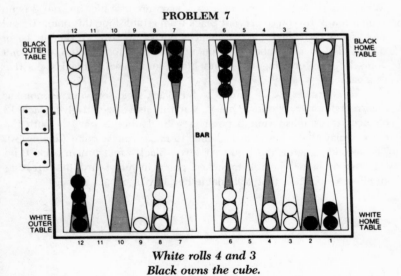

White rolls 4 and 3
Black owns the cube.

12

The correct play is to make White's 5 point. This formidable block you have created makes it very difficult for Black to escape. It would have been incorrect to have hit Black's blot on his 8 point. This would have given him an opportunity to make a second point in your board.

You should not be too concerned about escaping with your solitary man on Black's 1 point. Black will have to be very lucky in order to prevent this. Now that your board is so dangerous, the additional blots that Black may have to leave in his attempt to contain this man will expose him to being gammoned.

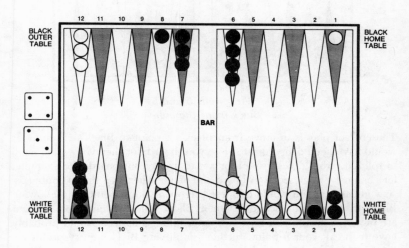

● ● ●

PROBLEM 8

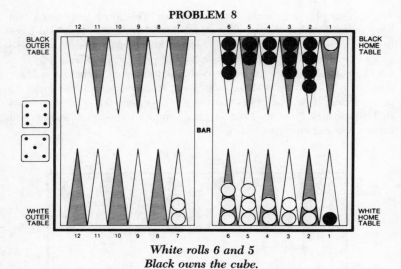

White rolls 6 and 5
Black owns the cube.

The correct play is to move from Black's 1 point to Black's 12 point. It would have been dangerous to close your board, for then you would need to roll a 6 rather quickly in order not to break your board. For example, let's assume you closed your board and on your next roll threw double 5s. As you can see, you would be forced to open your 6 point, thus allowing Black to enter and escape. Even if Black failed to enter on his first attempt, you would still need a 6, and, failing this, you would probably have to break your 5 point, further simplifying Black's entry problems. You might even be forced to leave a blot there, in which case Black should redouble.

An additional benefit you derive by not closing your board (although secondary in value to the advantage we just discussed) is that by being able to move, Black will be forced to break his own board. If, while bearing off, you leave a blot that is hit, your re-entry will be much easier than it would have been had his board remained intact.

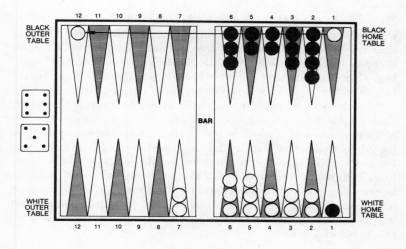

• • •

PROBLEM 9

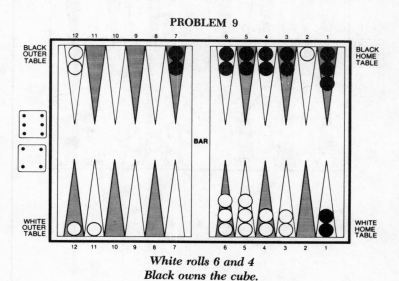

White rolls 6 and 4
Black owns the cube.

15

The correct play is to make White's bar point. This effectively blocks your opponent's escape with the exception of the roll of 1 and 6 (17 to 1 against). Without this roll Black is forced to break his position on his side of the table. Not only will he have to break, but he will possibly leave a blot which you will have an opportunity to hit. Having a third man of Black's will certainly increase your chances of winning a gammon.

If you choose to move out of Black's board, his chances of winning, although still not very good, are vastly increased. For example, the rolls of 6 and 5 or 6 and 4, which would hit one of your blots (assuming you moved the 6 and 4 to Black's 12 point), could prove disastrous for you. Double 6s would also be effective in helping Black's cause. On the other hand, with the play of making your bar point only the roll of double 1s should cause you any consternation. Even with this perfect roll, which would enable Black to move from your 1 point to your 2 point and put you on the bar, by moving his 3 point to his 2 point, he would still need two 6s before you were able to escape.

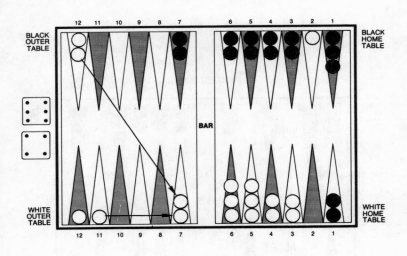

16

PROBLEM 10

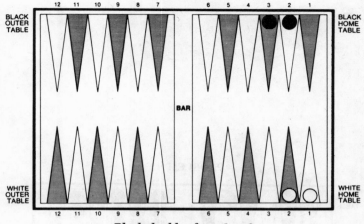

Black doubles from 1 to 2
Should White accept?

Yes. In order to show you why you must accept the double, we must assume that you will play this exact position 36 times.

According to the laws of probability, if you were to accept the double and play this game 36 times, 25 times Black would win, giving you a minus score of 50 (25 × 2). Eleven times he would fail to bear off both of his men (any roll with an ace) and thus you would win 22 points (11 × 2). Your net score at the end of 36 games would be minus 28 (50–22).

On the other hand if you declined the double all 36 times, your net loss would be 36. Therefore you lose 8 points *less* by accepting the double.

This theory holds true regardless of the number showing on the doubling block (whether you are doubled from 1 to 2, 2 to 4, 4 to 8, etc.).

● ● ●

17

PROBLEM 11

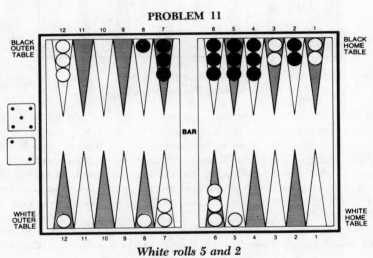

White rolls 5 and 2
White owns the cube.

18

The correct move is to make your 5 point. It is much too early to hit Black's blot on his 8 point and cover your 5 point by moving a man from your bar. This play would leave blots on your bar, 8, and on Black's 3 point, any one of which, if hit, could prove disastrous for you. You must build a better board and then hope to hit a blot. The odds are very much in your favor that Black will be forced to leave another blot, perhaps several, before the conclusion of this game.

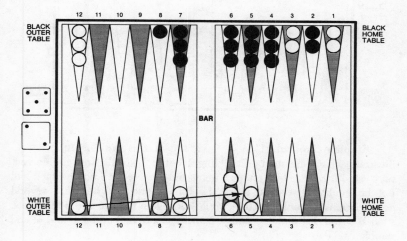

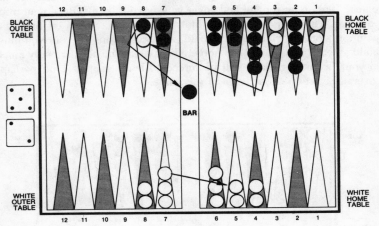

Examine Problem 11-A. I have shown this position in order to illustrate what I meant by "building a better board." Now the correct play is to hit Black's blot on his 8 point and make your 5 point. Black will not be unable to escape unless he rolls 3 and 6. There are several combinations he could roll that would cause him to have additional blots, such as 1 and 3, 1 and 4, 1 and 5, 2 and 4, 2 and 5, 3 and 4, 3 and 5, and double 3s.

• • •

PROBLEM 12

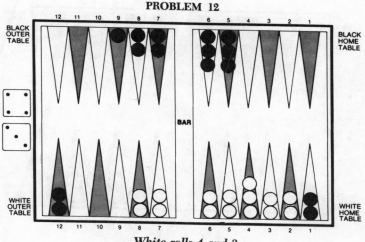

White rolls 4 and 3
Black owns the cube.

The correct play is to move both men from your bar point to your 4 and 3 points. You are not trying to contain Black's men on your 1 point. To the contrary, you wish they weren't there. You will not lose this game in a race—only by exposing a blot that is hit. By leaving two men on your 8 point, if you are forced to expose a blot in your attempt to enter these last two men, Black will be able to hit only with the roll of 6 and 1 (17 to 1 against). On the other hand, if you had used the 4 and 3 to bring the two men from your 8 point into your board, and if you were subsequently forced to leave a blot while attempting to bring your men in from your bar point (this would occur with the roll of 6 and 4, 6 and 5, and double 5's), your opponent would then have 11 chances out of 36 to hit—a big difference between that and the 2 out of 36 with the correct move.

21

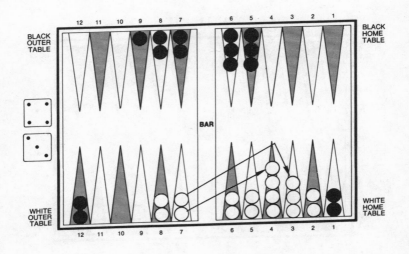

• • •

PROBLEM 13

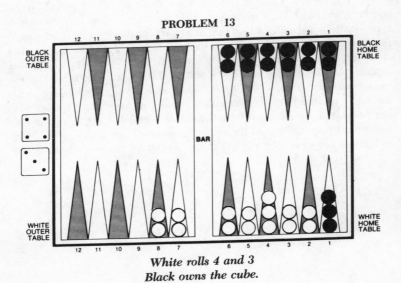

White rolls 4 and 3
Black owns the cube.

The correct play is to move both men from your 8 point to your 5 and 4 points. This position is vastly different from Problem 12. By preventing Black's escape with one of his men from your 1 point, you are forcing him to break his board on his next roll with anything but double 6s. As a result, in the event you are forced to leave a blot which in turn is hit, you will not have a closed board facing you.

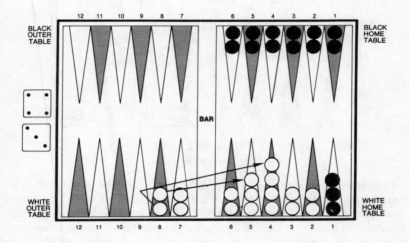

• • •

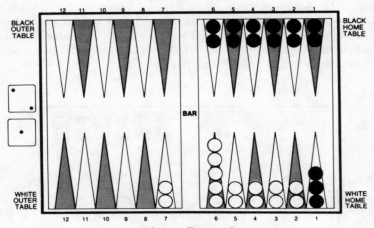

White rolls 2 and 1
Black owns the cube.

The correct play is to move two men from White's 6 point to White's 5 and 4 points. Although you could have safely entered your men from your bar point, by maintaining it you force Black to break his board with the rolls of 6 and 1, 6 and 2, 6 and 3, 6 and 4, and 6 and 5, which, had you moved your men from your bar point, would have permitted Black to escape with a man and thus be able to maintain his closed board.

It's true that by not bringing your men into your board you have created the possibility of having to leave a blot on your next roll. However, since the only rolls that will cause this to occur are 6 and 5 or double 5s (11 to 1 against), the possible gain certainly seems to justify this small risk.

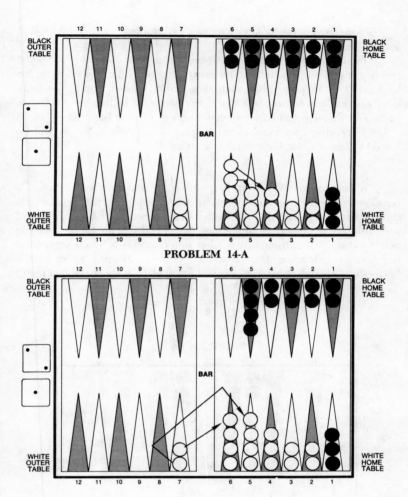

PROBLEM 14-A

25

Before moving on, look for a moment at Problem 14-A: White rolls 2 and 1—Black owns the cube.

Now it is correct to move both men from your bar point to your 6 and 5 points. You gain nothing by preventing Black from playing 6s, for he has no 6s to play other than those from your 1 point. The only numbers that can cause Black to destroy his board further are double 4s or 3s, and this will still happen even if you clear your bar point.

By entering your men, as you have, it is unlikely that you will be forced to leave a blot for several rolls, if at all.

To summarize: When it is possible to maintain comfortably a position that will cause your opponent to destroy or further weaken his threat, then you should do so. You should not when the gain is small and your risks are increased, as in the case of 14-A. (By maintaining your bar point you are not causing any further deterioration of Black's position, but merely extending the possibility of being forced to expose a blot—slight though it may be—as you attempt to enter these two men.)

● ● ●

PROBLEM 15

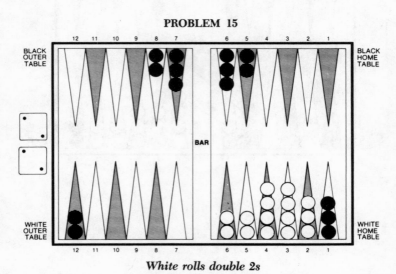

White rolls double 2s
Black owns the cube.

26

The correct play is to move two men from your 6 point to your 4 point and two men from your 5 point to your 3 point. The result of these moves is that you have eliminated the possibility of having to leave a blot on your next roll and minimized the chances of this for the next few rolls.

If you were to bear two men off your 4 point, on your succeeding roll, the combination of 6 and 5 or 5 and 4 would force you to leave two blots.

In general, when bearing off, and your opponent holds your 1 point, there is less likelihood of being forced to leave a blot when you have several men on few points than it is when you have few men on several points.

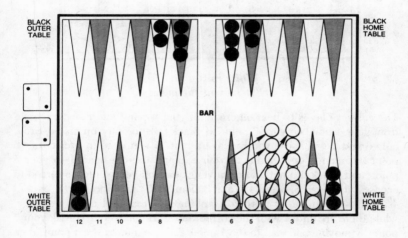

• • •

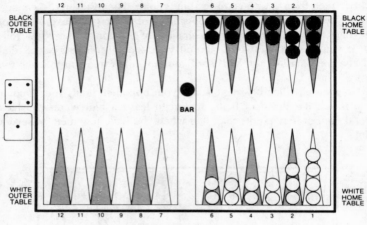

White rolls 4 and 1
Black owns the cube.

The correct play is to bear one man off your 4 point and move one man from your 4 point to your 3 point. If Black fails to enter on his next roll, only 6 and 2 will cause you to leave a blot. If you were to break your 6 point by moving one man 4 to your 2 point and one man 1 to your 5 point, and Black did not enter, on your next roll you would be forced to expose with 6 and 5, 6 and 4, 6 and 3, 5 and 4, 5 and 3, double 6s, 5s, and 4s. This adds up to 13 possible combinations that will cause exposure, while there are only 2 with the correct move. If you were to break your 5 point by moving one man to the 1 point and one man to the 4 point, then you would expose with 6 and 1, 5 and 1, double 6s, 5s, and 4s—seven combinations in all. This is better than moving from the 6 point, but hardly correct when you can make a move that will leave only 2 possibilities.

It is true that by breaking your 6 point, if Black enters, he is out of your hair for good; whereas, by breaking your 4 point, if he enters, you still must get your men past him. If this occurs, only the roll of 6 and 2 will cause a blot. This slight possibility should not in any way influence the decision to choose the move that you did.

28

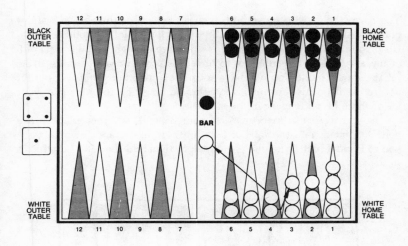

• • •

PROBLEM 17

White rolls 2 and 1
Black owns the cube.

29

The correct play is to move both men off your 6 point to your 5 and 4 points. This eliminates any possibility of having a blot on your next roll. Black, on his next turn—unless he is fortunate enough to roll a total of 5 or under—will be forced either to break his board or your 1 point. If he breaks your 1 point, you will have several combinations that will permit you to point on his remaining blot, thus forcing him to enter past your men where he no longer will be a threat.

If you were to bear a man off your 3 point, whether Black broke your 1 point or not, the rolls of double 6s, 4s, and 6 and 5 would force you to leave a blot. If he chose to break it, then add the roll of double 5s to the list.

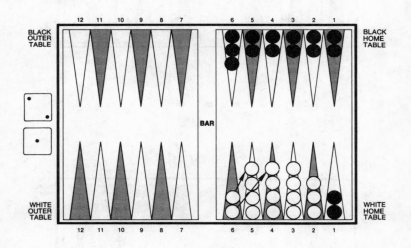

30

PROBLEM 18

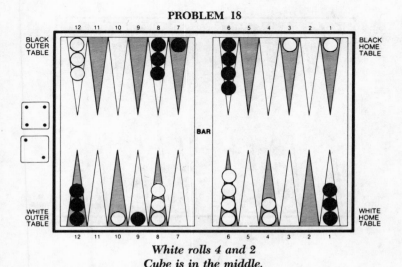

White rolls 4 and 2
Cube is in the middle.

The correct play is to make Black's 5 point. Now that you have this sound and solid position in Black's board you can turn your attention elsewhere. If your blot on your 10 point is not hit (even if it were, it certainly wouldn't hurt you much), you will have several combinations with which to make your bar or 5 points, thus making Black's hopes of winning rather dim.

In no way would it have been correct to make any move that would have hit either of Black's blots. A fourth man in your board would give Black the opportunity to make a second point, thus giving him the necessary ingredients to play a back game.

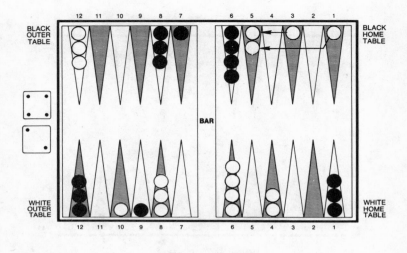

• • •

PROBLEM 19

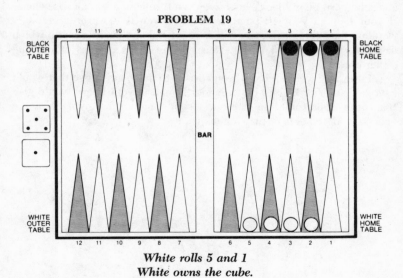

White rolls 5 and 1
White owns the cube.

32

The correct play is to bear one man from your 5 point and move one man from the 3 point to the 2 point. Assuming that Black does not bear off all three of his men on his turn, by using the ace to move from the 3 to the 2 point you increase your chances of bearing off your remaining three men by 25 percent. This is because you have given yourself the added possibility of winning with double 2s as well as double 3s, 4s, 5s, and 6s.

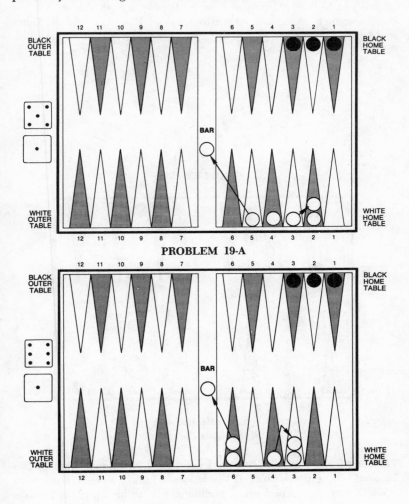

PROBLEM 19-A

33

Examine Problem 19-A. How do you play 6 and 1? Once again you must give yourself the most possible chances to bear your remaining three men off in one roll. By moving as you did, you include double 3s with double 6s, 5s, and 4s as numbers that can win for you (assuming, of course, that Black has not borne off his three men before it's your turn to roll). Try some other play of the ace and you will see that none will permit you to bear off your remaining three men with double 3s. It is these seemingly innocuous moves that win or lose many games. Don't worry, you'll soon recognize all of them. Backgammon really is beautiful, isn't it!

• • •

PROBLEM 20

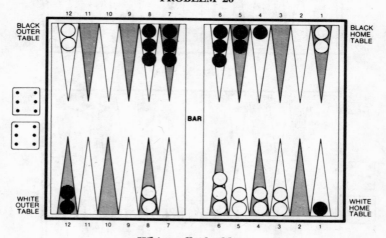

White rolls double 6s
Black owns the cube.

The correct move is to make your 1 point with your 2 men from Black's 12 point hitting Black's blot. If Black does not enter on his roll (25 to 11 against), you hope to pick up his additional blot on his 4 point or perhaps

34

close your board. If you are able to hit a second blot, you would then probably have the opportunity to escape and move around the board before Black is able to enter his men. You might even, as mentioned above, close your board. Then, assuming you could escape from Black's home board without having to open your home board, you would most likely win a gammon.

If Black enters, but is not able to make his 4 point (only 2 and 2, 2 and 3, 2 and 4 can accomplish this), you will still have a chance to hit the blot there. Failing this, or including it, you will be able to hit his blot on your 2 point (or your bar in the event his roll is 2 and 5 and he elects to move to your bar point). If Black rolls 2 and 6, he will be forced to leave an additional blot.

Alternatively, had you made your bar and 2 points, thus making a prime, Black would have 28 out of 36 chances to make his 4 point. If he succeeded in doing that, his position would be so strong that unless you were able to escape with a man on your next roll (2 and 6 only), or roll double 1s or 2s which would allow you to move to Black's 3 point, he should redouble and you should decline. Note: assuming that you made the prime and that Black then made his 4 points, there are only 7 numbers that you could roll that would not force you to break your prime—double 1s, 2s, 6, 5, 2 and 6, and 2 and 1.

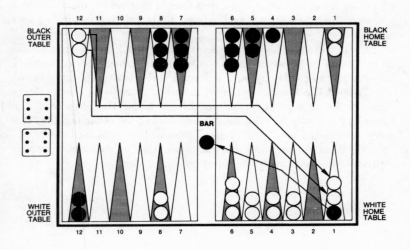

35

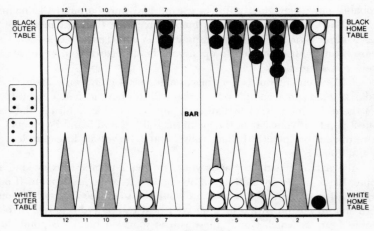

White rolls double 6s
Black owns the cube.

The correct move is to make your bar and 2 points (making a prime). The important thing in this position is that you must not prevent Black from advancing his men. Unless Black rolls double 6s, 6 and 1, 6 and 2, 2 and 1, or double 1s, he will be forced to break his board, thus facilitating your escape.

If you were to make your 1 point, hitting Black's blot, the odds are 25 to 11 that he will not enter. You would then quickly need some 1s, followed just as quickly by 6s, in order to avoid breaking your own board.

True, if Black rolls double 2s, 2 and 3, or 2 and 4, he would be forced to break a point on his side of the table. The chances of this happening are only 5 in 36. Bear in mind, also, the other numbers that enter—2 and 1, 2 and 5, and 2 and 6 are excellent rolls for Black.

All things taken into consideration, this is one time (directly contrasted to Problem 20) you must not hit!

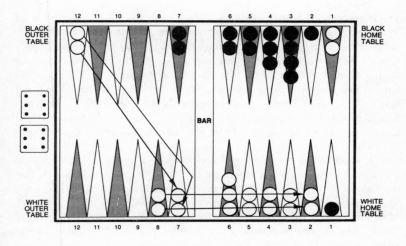

• • •

PROBLEM 22

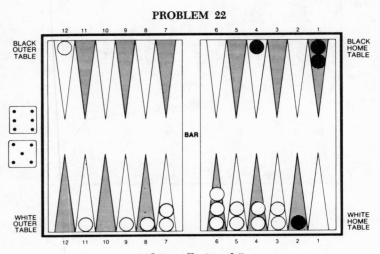

White rolls 6 and 5
White owns the cube.

The correct move is to hit Black's blot on your 2 point and move 1 man from your 6 point to your 1 point. Your main objective is to force Black to hit one of your men so you can have the opportunity to pick up Black's blot on Black's 4 point. It is not impossible to win this game without hitting Black's second blot, but the odds are against it. With Black's second man, however, you become a big favorite to win. You should not fear a Black roll of 2 and 6. In this event only the rolls of double 1s, 6 and 2, and double 6s will prevent you from hitting one of Black's two blots. Even then Black will still need to be very fortunate to get both of his men to safety.

It would have been wrong to have made a prime by moving from Black's 12 point to White's 8 point and then move some other 6. This play would give Black an opportunity to save his blot on his 4 point. Nor would it have been correct to have made your 2 point, hitting Black's blot. This makes it that much more difficult for Black to enter your board and hit one of your men, which you wish to accomplish. If Black fails to enter on his roll, you must attempt to leave both of your blots in your inner board.

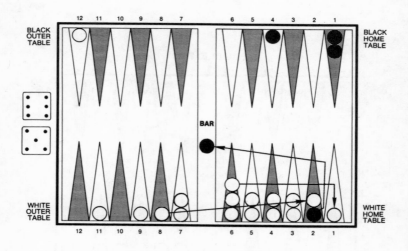

● ● ●

38

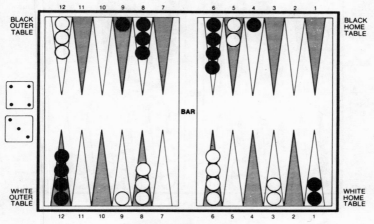

White rolls 4 and 3
Doubling cube is in the middle.

The correct move is to make White's 5 point. This gives you a position that is so strong that unless Black rolls double 3s or double 6s on his next roll, you should double. The fact that you possess an advanced point in Black's board makes it unlikely that you will find it difficult to escape when you wish.

The move of hitting Black's blot on Black's 9 point and continuing that man to Black's 12 point increases his chances of improving his position. Now the rolls of 5 and 4, double 5s, 4 and 3, and double 1s are immediately beneficial, plus rolls such as 5 and 1, 5 and 3, 2 and 1, and 2 and 3 that permit him to hit your blot on his 5 point, perhaps forcing you to hit a fourth man, which might give him the opportunity to play a back game.

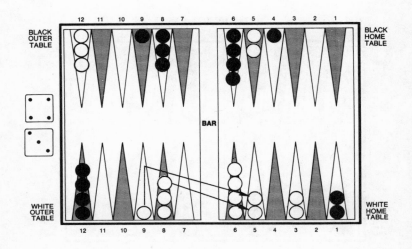

• • •

PROBLEM 24

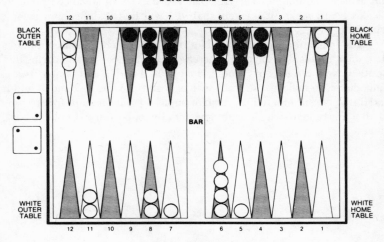

White rolls double 2s
White owns the cube.

The correct play is to make your 4 point, 5 point, and move one man from your 11 point to your 9 point.

You are much too far behind in the race to move to Black's 3 point. You must plan to build your board and hope to hit a blot as Black is bearing off.

With your men on Black's 3 point, he will have very little difficulty in entering his men safely, and the probabilities of his leaving a blot will be greatly reduced. True, a roll of double 6s would force him to leave a blot on his 9 point, but it also forces him to leave a blot on his 3 point if you stay back on Black's 1 point.

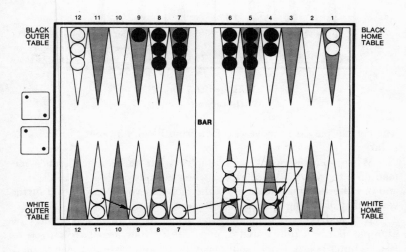

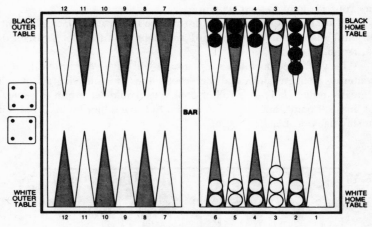

White rolls 5 and 4
White owns the cube.

The correct play is to move one man from Black's 3 point to Black's 12 point.

When your opponent has no builders left on his high points—one man does the work of two, except when he rolls double 1s, 2s, 3s, or 6 and 3. Offsetting this, however, is the fact that your board is still intact versus that of having opened your 6 point.

It would be wrong to move both men from Black's 3 point. For example, if Black rolls 6 and 3, and both of your men have moved to Black's outer board, Black would bear a 6 off and move one man to his 3 point. You would then have 11 chances to roll a 2 which would hit his blot. On the other hand, if you still had a man on his 3 point, he would be forced to hit this blot. You would then be able to hit his man on his 3 point with 15 combinations. Any 3 (11), 1 and 2 (2), and 6 and 2 (2). Basically similar statistics would hold true if Black rolled 4 and 3 or 3 and

42

2. Now take the roll of 6 and 5. By leaving one man on Black's 3 point you would be able to hit one of his blots with 2s, 3s, 4s, or 5s (33 chances). If on the other hand you did not have that man on his 3 point, then only 4s and 5s, double 2s, and 2 and 3 would hit (23 chances). Your gain is almost the same when Black rolls 5 and 4.

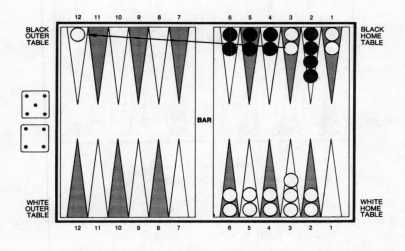

• • •

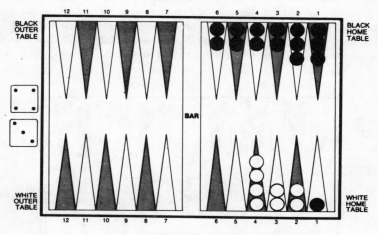

White rolls 4 and 3
Black owns the cube.

The correct move is to bear one man off White's 4 point and move one man from White's 4 point to White's 1 point, hitting Black's blot. Your blot will be hit 11 out of 36 times. However, of those 11 times, double 1s, 1 and 2, and 1 and 3 will cause Black to break his board. With the exception of double 1s, you will have a shot at hitting whichever blot he chooses to leave.

With the alternate move of bearing one man off your 4 point and one man off your 3 point, Black will have the same number of chances to hit your blot. If he does, none of these 11 combinations will cause him to break his board (versus 5 out of 11 with the move of hitting on your 1 point).

There are other things to be taken into consideration. I am going to explain all of them now in some depth, because positions that are similar but not quite identical constantly arise. Therefore you should be aware of all of the facts that may influence your decision.

I will start by discussing what will happen when Black misses your blot. When you have hit him on your 1 point one of two things can occur: he can enter on your 5 or 6 point, thus ending your problems, or he can fail to enter, in which case the worst that can happen is that you leave a blot after your next roll. By this time, however, you should have enough men off to win even if you are hit. In the event you are not hit, you will have a good chance of winning a gammon.

Now let's see what happens if you bear 2 men off instead of hitting on the 1 point, again assuming that Black misses your blot. If his roll contains a 6, he is forced to leave your board, again ending your worries (11 chances versus 20 when you hit on the 1 point). If on the other hand he is able to remain on your 1 point, there are several rolls that could force you to leave 2 blots, such as 6 and 5, 6 and 4, and 5 and 4.

All things taken into consideration, you can see that it's quite obvious which is the correct play.

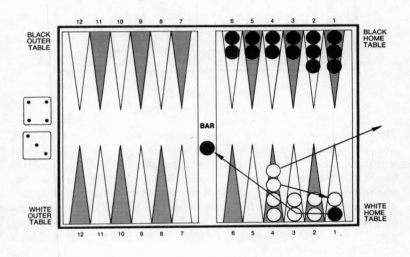

• • •

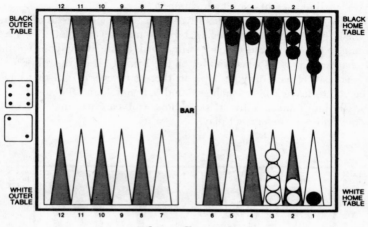

White rolls 6 and 2
Black owns the cube.

The correct move is to bear one man from your 3 point and one man from your 2 point. This appears on the surface to resemble Problem 26. It is vastly different, however. The fact that Black does not have a closed board, plus the fact that if your resulting blot on your 2 point is not hit, you will quite likely win a gammon, are the determining factors in your decision to bear your man from your 2 point rather than hit Black's blot on your 1 point. There is also the possibility that you will win a triple game. Black might roll 3 and 2 or double 2s followed by your double 3s or better.

True, by bearing two men off, you may be forced to leave two blots on your subsequent roll. No importance should be placed on this possibility because most likely Black will either be forced to leave your 1 point (any 6, 5, or double 4s), or by choice in order perhaps to save a gammon or backgammon. Added to this is the fact that if Black does not hit or is not forced to leave your 1 point, his board will have one and perhaps two fewer points for you to be concerned with.

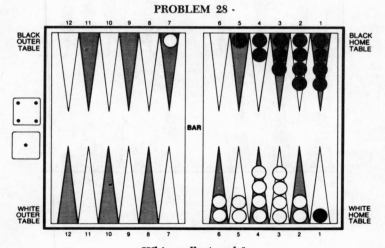

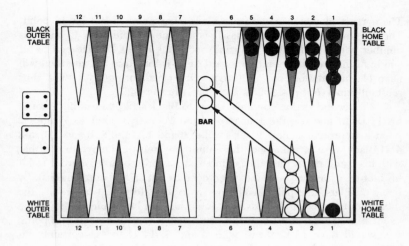

PROBLEM 28 ·

White rolls 4 and 1
Black owns the cube.

The correct play is to move from Black's bar point to Black's 12 point. The reason that you have exposed your blot to double 6s is that this number will probably win the game for Black unless he is forced to hit you in his mad dash around the board. If he is forced to hit, you then will have 11 combinations out of 36 that will hit his blot on his 5 point, thus reëstablishing your position as a big favorite to win.

The second reason you must move to Black's 12 point rather than to his 11 point and use the 1 to move from White's 3 point to White's 2 point is to protect against Black's roll of 6 and 1, 6 and 2, 6 and 3, 6 and 4. If Black were to roll any of those numbers, he would move to your bar with his 6 and move the other number in his inner board. In order to hit his blot on your bar you would then need to roll a 7 (6 combinations). By being on Black's 12 point, assuming any of the aforementioned rolls, the minimum number of chances you would have to hit would be 12. In the event Black rolls 6 and 1 or 6 and 2 and moves to your 8 point or 9 point, you would have 15 chances; with 6 and 3, 14 chances—certainly far better than the 7 chances offered by staying on Black's 11 point.

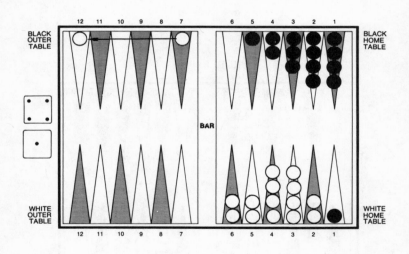

48

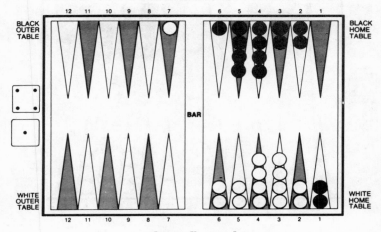

White rolls 4 and 1
Black owns the cube.

The correct play is to move from Black's bar point to Black's 11 point, and from White's 3 point to White's 2 point.

In contrast to Problem 26, a roll of double 6s for Black will not make him a favorite to win unless he *is* able to hit your blot.

Assuming the worst—Black's roll of double 6s—and assuming that he moves one man from White's 1 point to Black's 6 point and 1 man from White's 1 point to White's bar, you will still be favored to win in a race, plus the fact that you still will have the chance of hitting Black's blot on your bar by rolling a 7.

Now let's consider what will happen in the more likely event of Black's rolling 6 and 5, 6 and 4, 6 and 3, 6 and 2, or 6 and 1.

With any of these rolls Black would be forced to move one man from White's 1 point to White's bar. Regardless of where Black chooses to move the remainder of his roll you will find that there is no number that you could roll that would not either bring your man on Black's 11 point to safety or that would not be able to hit either Black's blot in your outer board or his blot on your 1 point. Assuming the worst, the roll with which you hit Black's blot on your 1 point (leaving a blot of your own), your chances are still 25 to 11 not to be hit. Even if you were hit, you would still be favored to win.

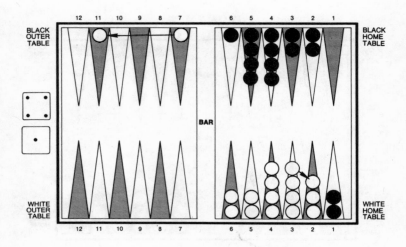

• • •

PROBLEM 30

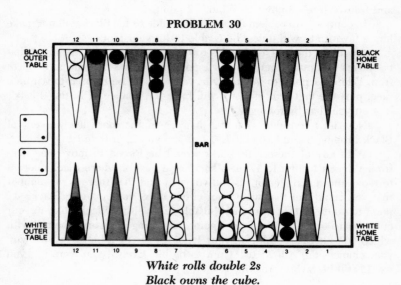

White rolls double 2s
Black owns the cube.

The correct play is to move two men from Black's 12 point to White's 11 point, one man from White's bar point to White's 5 point, and one man from White's 6 point to White's 4 point. It would not have been correct to move from Black's 12 point to White's 9 point, the reason being that you are not trying to block Black's escape from your 3 point. You are so far ahead in the race that your only problem now is to avoid problems in bringing your men into your home board. If you put your men on your 9 point, Black's men on your 3 point, you will have become a block which will restrict their safe movement into your home board. Any future roll that contains a 6 or a 1 (except double 1s) will prevent you from moving these two men into your board. In effect, this means that each time you roll you will not be favored to enter these men safely.

On the other hand, what happens to your men when you leave them on your 11 point? The best that might occur is that you roll some number with 6s and 5s or 4s, double 3s or 2s, which will bring both men to the safety of your bar and/or inner points.

The worst that could happen is that after several unsuccessful attempts to move them in without leaving a blot, you would be forced to leave a blot on your 11 point. This blot will then be exposed only to a 6 and 2 or 5 and 3 (4 chances out of 36).

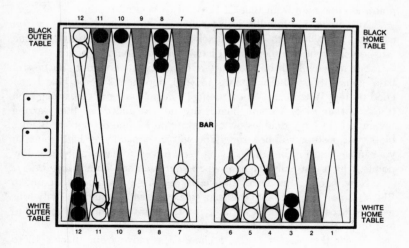

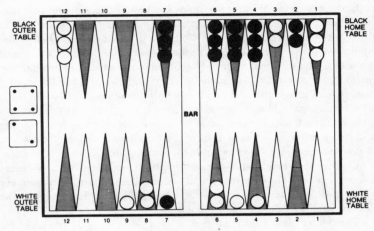

White rolls 4 and 2
White owns the cube.

The correct play is to move one man from Black's 1 point to Black's 3 point and one man from Black's 12 point to White's 9 point.

Any move that hits Black's blot on your bar point is incorrect. You cannot possibly hope to contain Black's lone blot, while at the same time escape with your five men from Black's formidable home board.

You have both of the necessary requirements to conduct a successful back game—two valuable points in your opponent's home board and good timing. When I say "good timing" I mean that your remaining men (those not in Black's home board) are not advanced, so that barring several sets of large doubles, when and if you hit one or more of Black's blots your position will be strong. You will have made your high points in your inner board rather than having been forced to have made your low points, which is usually the case when your men are too advanced.

Now, back to the correct move: By moving from Black's 1 point to Black's 3 point, you enable this man to escape with 5s and 6s. Only four men are necessary in Black's board, and this extra man may be needed to help build your own board.

As for the play of the 4, I choose the move from Black's 12 to White's 9 point. Although not disastrous, a roll of double 2s for Black would be unpleasant, for he would be forced into an unattractive position in his home board.

It would not have been incorrect had you used the 4 to make your 5 point.

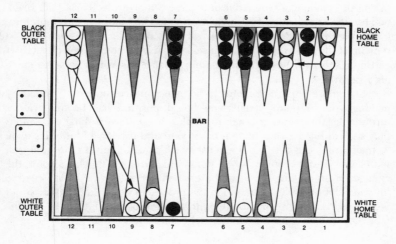

• • •

PROBLEM 32

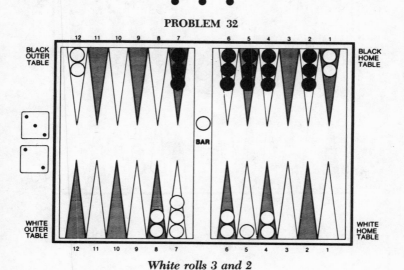

White rolls 3 and 2
White owns the cube.

The correct play is to enter on Black's 3 point and move one man from White's bar point to White's 5 point. There is almost no chance for you to win this game in a race. Your only hope is that while bearing off, Black will be forced to leave a blot, which you hit. The point to hold, therefore, is Black's 1 point. From there you will be a threat as long as you wish to remain. If, on the other hand, you make Black's 3 point, your chances of getting a shot will be far less (assuming that Black will be able to make his 1 point).

One more important factor to be taken into consideration is that by making your 5 point your home board position has become rather formidable, thus causing Black to think twice before making a frivolous play such as hitting your blot on his 3 point and leaving a blot of his own. Actually, the odds are 5 to 4 against Black's making his 3 point (any roll with a 6 or 5—20 chances out of 36). If you had made Black's 3 point, the chances of his making the 1 point are much better. Also, if he is forced to hit your blot on his 1 point, and in the process of doing so leaves a blot of his own (this would happen only with a roll of 6 and 2), there is still the fact that your board leaves much to be desired.

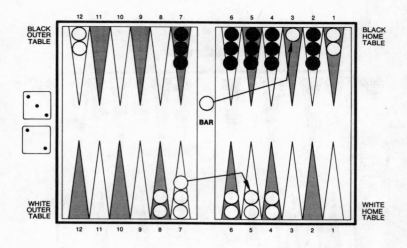

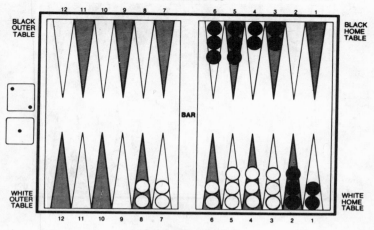

White rolls 2 and 1
Black owns the cube.

The correct play is to move one man from White's bar point to White's 5 point. By giving up your prime, you now force Black to break your 1 point with any roll that contains a 6 (except 5 and 6). This is something he desperately does not want to do since this would give you the opportunity to make your 1 point. Another reason for giving up your bar point rather than your 8 point is that if you are forced to leave a blot in your attempt to enter your remaining man from your 8 point, your opponent will have men on only one point that is in direct range (6 or less pips away) to hit with. If you choose to break your 8 point and subsequently are forced to leave a blot on your bar point, your opponent would have men on two points that would be bearing directly on this blot (therefore increasing his chances of hitting).

If you're asking why break your prime at all, the answer is this: on your next roll you must do so in any case (except with the roll of double 6s). By placing all of your odd men on the 3 point you will have increased the probability of leaving blots in the attempt to enter your remaining men.

By maintaining the prime, you also prevent Black from playing 6s, which, as you can see, are very bad for him. It's true that by breaking your bar point you allow him to escape with a five, but a five he can handle in his home board anyway.

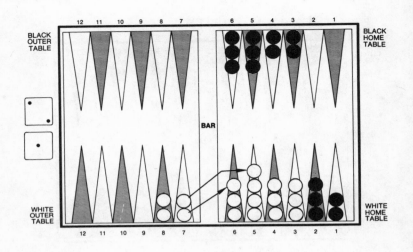

• • •

PROBLEM 34

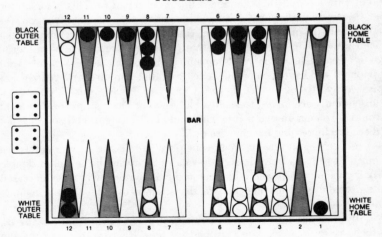

White rolls double 6s
Black owns the cube.

The correct play is to move both men from Black's 12 point to White's 1 point, hitting Black's blot. If Black does not enter on his next roll (25 to 11 against entering), you can do the following pleasant things on your next roll:

1. close your board (10 chances)
2. hit one of Black's blots (4 chances—with 6 and 2 you would close your board; therefore I have included those 2 chances above)
3. move your man on Black's 1 point to Black's 12 point (2 chances)
4. move to Black's bar point (4 chances)

There are other good rolls, the ramifications of which are complex because they revolve around the possibility of Black's not entering on his succeeding turn. This would include the rolls of 3 and 1, which would enable you to move one man to your bar point and one man to your 5 point. So, assuming Black does not enter, you will increase your chance of closing your board. With a 3 and 2 you would move from Black's 1 point to Black's 3 point and bring an additional builder into your home board on the 5 point.

Rather than go any further, let me say that the only bad roll is double 5s; only 5 and 4 or double 4s will not do some good.

Now let's assume Black enters on his next roll. If he rolls 2 and 5 (17 to 1 against), you will still have 17 chances to hit one of his blots, any one of which will more than likely win the game.

If he rolls 2 and 1, 2 and 3, 2 and 4, or 2 and 6, your plan should be to hit his blot on your 2 point—unless you are able to hit one of his blots in his outer board. You are a more than 3-to-1 favorite to accomplish this.

If Black rolls double 2s, well—*c'est la vie*—you've probably lost the game.

Now, however, let's investigate what might happen had you made the play of making your bar point and your 2 point.

Black would then have 24 numbers to make his bar. Your position would then be desperate, since you would need some miracles to get out of his now formidable trap.

Let's assume Black is unfortunate and does not make his bar; any roll for you that contains a 5 or 4 without a 6 will force you to break your prime, permitting him either to escape or hit any blot you may leave, depending on what you roll and how you elect to play it.

Although it might be enjoyable to continue an analysis of this problem, its solution is fairly cut and dried, and the time has come to move on.

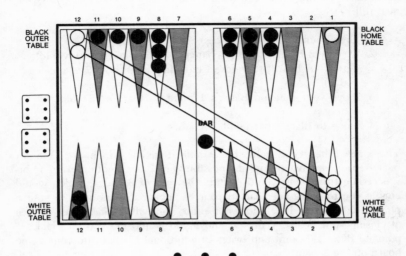

• • •

PROBLEM 35

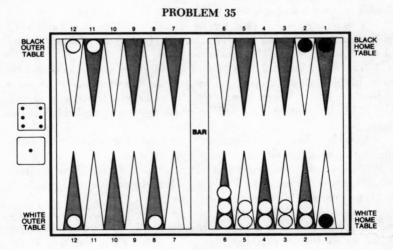

White rolls 6 and 1
White owns the cube.

The correct play is to move one man 1 from White's 2 point to White's 1 point, hitting Black's blot and one man from Black's 12 point to White's bar point. Your objective is to force Black to hit your blots, so that these men may reënter and pick up Black's blots on his board. You therefore disdain making a prime. Although it would most likely prevent you from losing a gammon, it would also minimize your chances of winning. This play would allow Black to eliminate his inner board blots if he rolled a 1.

The reason you did not make your 8 point is that in the event Black rolls a 1 or a 2 (hitting one of your blots) but cannot move from there, and you in turn roll a number that does not hit either of Black's men on his 1 or 2 points, you must have men in position to hit his blot in your board.

For example, assume you had made your 8 point and Black rolled 2 and 4 (entering on your 2 point and hitting your blot). If you now rolled 3 and 5, you would be unable to hit on your 2 point without breaking another point in your board, once again giving Black the opportunity to make his 1 point with the roll of an ace.

Before moving to the next problem, I would like to mention a point of interest. Since backgammon is not an exact science, it is difficult and sometimes impossible to make qualified statements regarding certain areas of play. One of these areas involves those games where your opponent has borne off several men and you then hit one of his men.

There are many factors which must be taken into consideration before making any assertions concerning your probabilities of winning or losing. Such as, how many men your opponent has borne off; on what points his remaining men are located, and, where your three extra men are (the men other than those needed for a closed board).

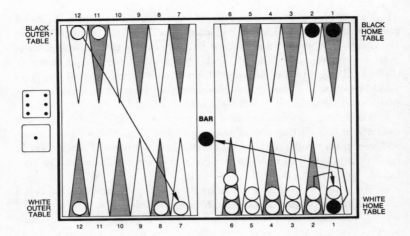

My experience has been that the break-even point occurs when my opponent has borne off eight men and his remaining men are located in such a position that when he resumes bearing off, he will not miss. This also assumes that my three odd men are favorably placed (in the high points in my game board), which should enable me to bear off at least two men before being forced to open my board.

PROBLEM 35-A

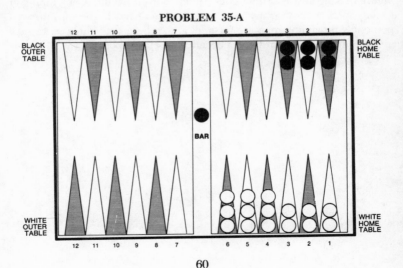

In contrast, look at Diagram B. It is unlikely that I will be able to bear any men off before I am forced to open my board (except with the roll of double 1s or 2 and 1). Thus, the pendulum has swung to Black so that he is probably favored to win more than 50 percent of the time.

PROBLEM 35-B

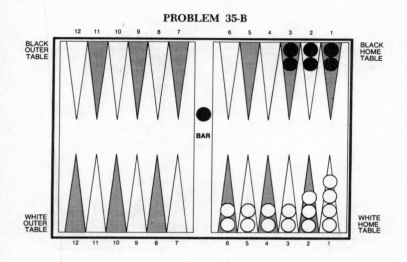

PROBLEM 35-C

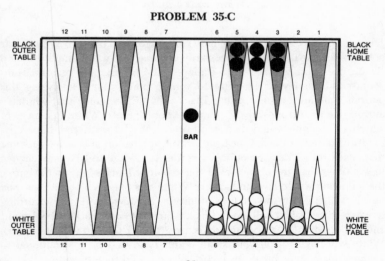

In Diagram 35-C, things are drastically different in Black's home board. Now, when Black resumes bearing off, he will probably miss several times. In a position such as this, you are well favored to win.

● ● ●

PROBLEM 36

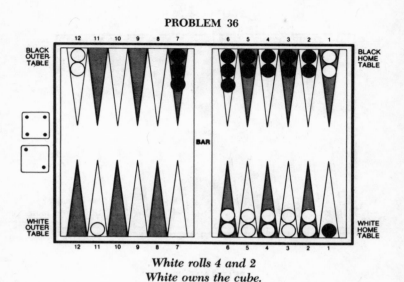

White rolls 4 and 2
White owns the cube.

The correct play is to move one man from Black's 12 point to White's bar point. It seems you have unnecessarily exposed a blot to being hit by a 6 (11 chances), for you could have played safe by bringing one man into your board from your 11 point to your 5 point. When analyzing this position, one must assume that if Black rolls a 6 (assuming that you have moved one man from your 11 point to your 5 point), White's chances of winning the game would then in all probability be restricted, hopefully, to hitting a blot as Black is bearing off. In explanation of this, let's assume that Black rolls 6 and something. In order for White to have any chance to win other than the chance of hitting a blot of Black's later in the game, the following would have to happen: White hits Black's blot with his men on Black's 12 point (the chances of hitting, of course, will vary according to where Black's blot will land). Black then must enter on White's 1 point and not be able to escape (the odds are 25 to 11 that he will not enter). White will have to roll very small numbers so that he is not forced to advance his men or break his board. Black would then have to roll large numbers (without a 6), thus forcing him to break his prime. White would then have to escape with his two men from Black's 1 point, and at the same time contain Black's blot on White's 1 point. There is more, but as you can see, White's chances of winning in this fashion are extremely remote.

Instead of moving from White's 11 point to White's 5 point, you move from Black's 12 point to White's bar. If Black rolls a 6, he will hit one, perhaps two or even three of your blots.

Unquestionably, if this happens, you will have exposed yourself to an increased probability of being gammoned. Commensurate with this are your increased chances of winning. Since you will be unable to move until you enter (this should take several rolls depending on how many of your blots Black picks up), you will not be forced to break your board. There is also the possibility of your still having a man on the bar if Black is forced to leave a blot while bearing off. This increases your chances of hitting.

Now that we have covered what might occur with both plays of the 4 and 2 when Black rolls a 6 and something, let's investigate the more likely occurrence when Black does not roll a 6.

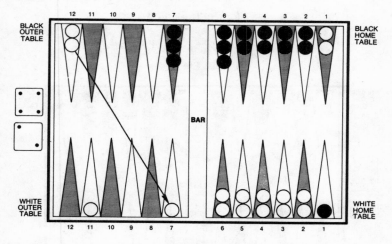

First, let's assume you moved one man to your bar point. Without a 6, Black will be forced to advance his men on his side of the table. If on your next roll you are able to cover your blot on your bar point (29 chances out of 36), giving you a prime, there will be a good likelihood of Black's being forced to break his prime on his next roll. The following diagrams illustrate a possible, and probable, progression of positions, assuming you had moved one man to White's bar point (excluding any roll of Black's that contains a 6).

PROBLEM 36-A

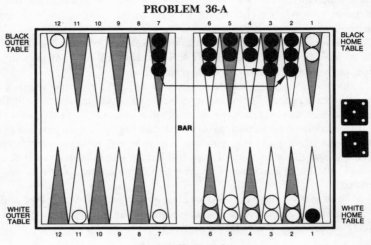

Black rolls 5 and 3

PROBLEM 36-B

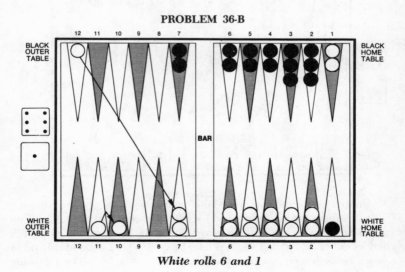

White rolls 6 and 1

64

At this point Black will be forced to break his prime with any roll except double 6s or 6 and 1 (11 to 1). If he were forced to break badly (this would happen with rolls such as double 2s, 3s, 4s, 5s, 5 and 4, 5 and 3, 6 and 5, etc.), you should redouble on the assumption that you will either escape with a 6 or be able to maintain your prime if you roll low numbers, and because Black will be weakened even more on his next roll.

Now lets see what happens with the safe play of moving from White's 11 point to White's 5 point (again assuming that Black does not roll a 6). He will still be forced to advance in his board, but now you will not have 29 out of 36 chances to make a prime—only double 3s (1 out of 36). True, Black could still lose the game, even if you don't make the prime, but the object of this discussion is to show that if you must assume that certain rolls cannot occur if you are to have any chance of winning, then you must make your moves based on that assumption and be able to take maximum advantage.

• • •

PROBLEM 37

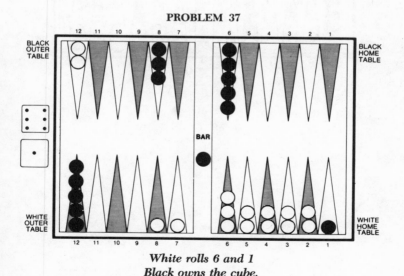

White rolls 6 and 1
Black owns the cube.

The correct play is to move one man from White's 8 point to White's 1 point, hitting Black's blot. You must try to prevent Black from establishing your 1 point. If you were to make your bar in lieu of hitting, Black would have 11 chances out of 36 to roll a 1, giving him a position from which he will still be able to win the game.

By hitting, Black must roll two 1s if he is to make your 1 point. If he hits your blot, you will have no difficulty in reëntering, and you should plan to keep hitting Black's blot on your 1 point until either you or he establish this point.

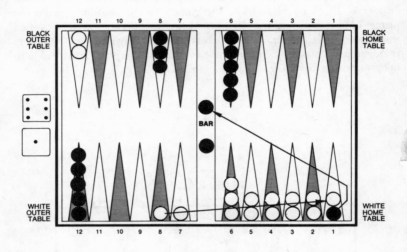

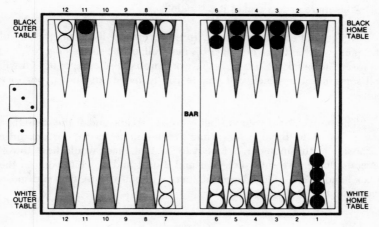

White rolls 3 and 1
Black owns the cube.

The correct play is to move from Black's bar to Black's 10 point and from Black's 12 point to White's 12 point. You must avoid hitting Black's blots, for to do so you would be delaying this forward progress, enabling him to maintain a threatening position in his home board.

By not hitting, Black will be forced to move into his inner board and eventually break his board while you are bringing your men around and into your home board. Therefore, when and if you do leave a blot while bearing off, Black's board will have been destroyed. You needn't worry about the blot that you have left exposed to being hit by a 1.

If hit, one of three things can happen:

1. You will fail to enter and Black will continue to be forced to move forward until he eventually opens one or two of the high points in his board, whereupon you simply reënter and resume your movement in preparation to bearing off. This is beneficial for you, for Black's board will be toothless.

2. You will enter and be forced to hit Black's blot on his 2 point. This is not as good, for in effect it is almost the same as if you had hit one of his blots on your previous roll. As I explained before, you do not wish to slow Black's progress. However, although you have been forced to hit

Black's blot, you also have been slowed down (as a result of having been hit). This more or less makes it a standoff.

3. You will enter and not hit. In this event the likely progression of the game will be: Black on either his next roll, or the succeeding roll, will be forced to break his board, easing your problem of escape; or you will roll some number which will enable you to move out under your own power.

The possibility of your not being able to escape and at the same time being forced to break your prime is so remote as to warrant little discussion at this moment. Suffice it to say that Black would have to roll several consecutive rolls such as 1 and 2 or 1 and 3, while you, on the other hand, were rolling large numbers without a 6. (A 6 would move your man out of Black's board.)

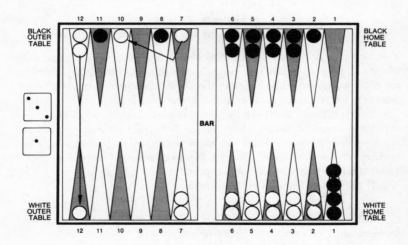

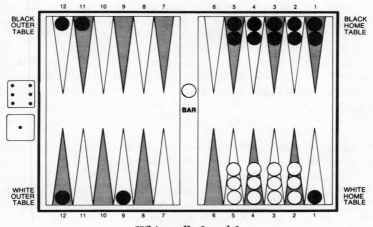

White rolls 6 and 1
Black owns the cube.

The correct play is to enter on Black's 6 point and move one man from White's 2 point to White's 1 point, hitting Black's blot. If Black fails to enter on his next roll (he will fail to do so 16 out of 36 times), you will have 29 chances to cover your blot on your 1 point. Of the remaining seven numbers, 6 and 1, 5 and 1, and double 5's will hit two additional blots of Black, putting three of his men on the bar, and a 6 and 5 will put a second man on the bar.

In short, in the event of entry failure by Black, you will have become a big favorite to win not only the game—but a gammon as well. Let's see what happens when Black is able to enter.

In the event Black rolls a 1 and hits your blot, the tide will unfortunately be turned in Black's favor. You will however still have some numbers that will keep disaster away from your door, depending on what Black's other number was. If his roll was 1 and 6 or 1 and 5 then his correct play would be to hit you on his 6 point, putting two of your men on the bar; with 1 and 1, 1 and 2, or 1 and 4, he should make some point in his outer board. Let's assume 3 and 1, however, in which case with 6 and 2, 6 and 3, 6 and 4, you would enter and once again hit Black's blot on your 1 point; 6 and 5, which enables you to enter and hit Black's blot on his 11 point; and double 6s, which enables you to hit the blot on Black's 12 point. With all of these numbers, Black will once again be in jeopardy of losing a double game if he fails to enter on his next roll. If you are unable to roll one of these combinations, Black should double and you should decline.

In the event Black is able to enter on your 6 point and not your 1 point, but does not roll double 6s or 6 and 5 (in this case he would hit your blot on his 6 point, creating a condition similar to the condition just discussed), your man on Black's 6 point will have several combinations that will hit one of Black's blots, which by necessity must still be exposed. This will enable you to move into your home board, or move to a position in your outer board where Black will have only one man left with which to hit.

Having covered all of the possibilities of what might happen when you hit on the 1 point, let's investigate the alternative. Your blot, whether left on Black's 6 point or bar point, will almost surely be hit. The burden will then be on you to enter before Black can make his 6 point. The least Black can be said to be favored to win is 25 to 11 (the chances of your entering on the 6 point). Contrast this with all of the possibilities above and it becomes obvious which play is more advantageous.

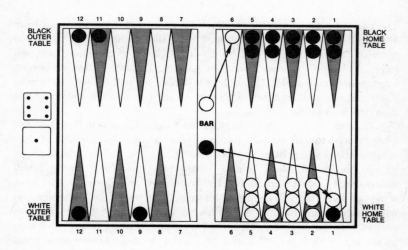

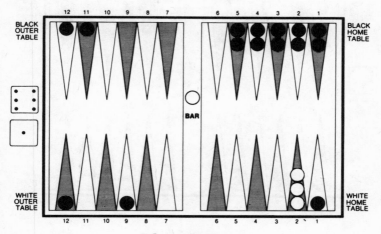

White rolls 6 and 1
Black owns the cube.

The correct play is to enter on Black's 6 point and move to Black's bar point. This problem is being shown following Problem 39 to demonstrate a direct contrast. Unless Black is able to pick up a second man, White is well-favored to win, even assuming Black will be able to close his board.

There is little point in discussing how the play would normally proceed. Black will keep hitting White's blot until he has closed his 6 point. (To avoid this, White would have to be tremendously lucky, for Black, even if hit, will have no difficulty in entering White's board.) After closing the board, Black eventually will be forced to open and allow White to enter. The odds are in favor of White's getting back to his home board and off more quickly than Black.

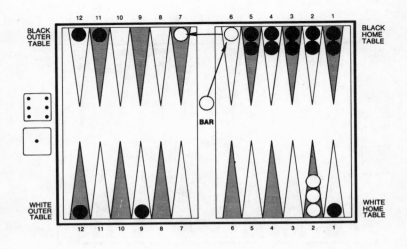

●   ●   ●

PROBLEM 41

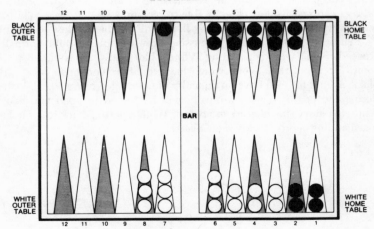

Should White double?
Cube is in the middle.

72

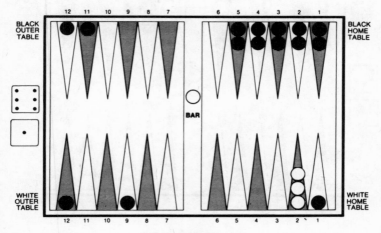

White rolls 6 and 1
Black owns the cube.

The correct play is to enter on Black's 6 point and move to Black's bar point. This problem is being shown following Problem 39 to demonstrate a direct contrast. Unless Black is able to pick up a second man, White is well-favored to win, even assuming Black will be able to close his board.

There is little point in discussing how the play would normally proceed. Black will keep hitting White's blot until he has closed his 6 point. (To avoid this, White would have to be tremendously lucky, for Black, even if hit, will have no difficulty in entering White's board.) After closing the board, Black eventually will be forced to open and allow White to enter. The odds are in favor of White's getting back to his home board and off more quickly than Black.

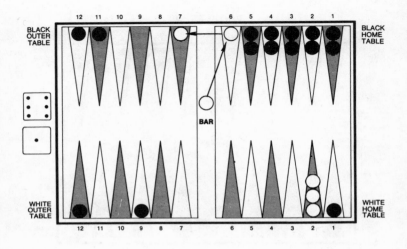

• • •

PROBLEM 41

Should White double?
Cube is in the middle.

Yes. Black's position is definitely not good—but it is not hopeless. If you were to play this same game 36 times to its conclusion without doubling, Black would certainly win several games. White, on the other hand, would probably win several gammons. So it becomes a problem of simple arithmetic to determine whether you should double. Examine the following figures, realizing that they are only probable and could vary a little in either direction.

First, assume you do not double, and play the same game 36 times:

18 times you win 1 point	+ 18
9 times you win 2 points	+ 18
(a gammon)	+ 36
9 times you lose 1 point	− 9

Assume you do not accept a redouble:

Net result   + 27

Now, assume you double and your opponent declines all 36 times (it would be correct to decline):

36 times you win 1 point   + 36

Since not all of your opponents will decline, what happens when one accepts?

18 times you win 2 points	+ 36
9 times you win 4 points	+ 36
(a gammon)	+ 72
9 times you lose 2 points	− 18

Assume you do not accept a redouble:

Net result   + 54

As you can see, not only should you double but you hope your opponent accepts. If you were now to say to yourself, "How can I possibly become so experienced as to be able to judge or predict that 9 out of 36 games I will win a gammon and 9 times I will lose the game?" You can't—nor can I.

What you can do is realize that unless you are able to win more than twice as many gammons as games, you will lose (assuming you were to play the same game X number of times); then you must double.

For example, in those same 36 games, instead of predicting that you

73

will win 18 at 1 point, 9 at 2 points (a gammon), and lose 9 at 1 point, for a net of + 27 points, change that to 24 at 1 point, 6 at 2 points, and lose 6 at 1 point for a net of + 30; you still don't win as many points as when you double.

By the way, it doesn't matter whether you use the number 36 or 50 or 100 as a determining number of games to play. I choose 36 out of habit, since that is the number you will always use in determining probabilities as applied to rolls of the dice.

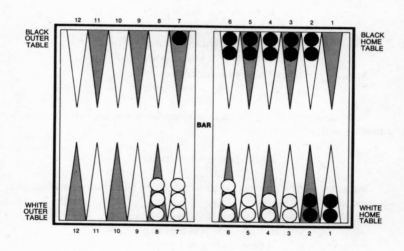

• • •

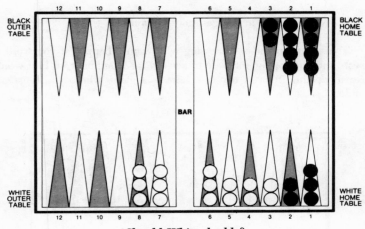

Should White double?
Cube is in the middle.

The answer is no. Once again I will give you a problem which illustrates a direct contrast to the preceding problem.

As I explained in Problem 41, the determining factor in whether to double is the ratio of probable gammons to probable losses.

In this game, whether it's played 36 times or 360 times, you would have to be very unfortunate to lose even 5 percent of the time. On the other hand, I would be extremely conservative in saying that you will win a gammon 25 percent of the time.

Let's use our simple arithmetic once again. This time we'll do it on the basis of 100 games (I choose 100 rather than 36 in order to avoid fractions).

Assume you do not double:

70% of the time you win 1 point	+ 70
25% of the time you win 2 points	
(a gammon)	+ 50
5% of the time you lose 1 point	− 5
Net result	+115

Assume you double:

You win 100 games at 1 point $+100$

There is no point in discussing what would happen if you were to double and your opponent were to accept; for Houdini at his best would have to decline. As you can see, here is a game where you must not double.

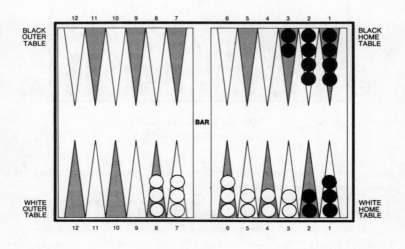

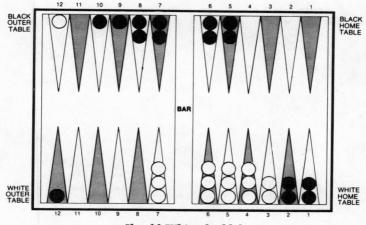

Should White double?
Cube is in the middle.

No. White should not double. Continuing in the vein of Problems 41 and 42, this problem is shown because it is dramatically opposed not only in Black's position on the board but also in the probable outcome of the game.

No longer are you a prohibitive favorite to win a large majority of the time. To the contrary, Black has all of the necessary elements for a successful backgame (two valuable points in your board and the proper timing, so when and if you do leave a blot, his board will be formidable and eager to accept it). Therefore it's good common sense that you don't want to increase the stakes unless it is probable that you will win more than 50 percent of the time.

● ● ●

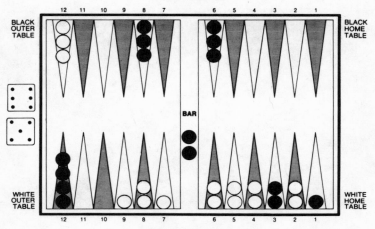

White rolls 6 and 5
Black owns the cube.

The correct play is to move one man from White's bar point to White's 1 point, hitting Black's blot, and one man from White's 9 point to White's 4 point.

It is of the utmost importance that you prevent Black from establishing your 1 point. You moved from the 9 point to the 4 point rather than from Black's 12 point to your 8 point for two reasons: to increase your chances of covering your 1 point in the event Black does not hit your blot there, or to be able to hit him again if he does hit your blot.

You should have no fear of being hit, for you will have no problems in reëntering. However, if Black is able to establish your 1 point, instead of your winning a probable gammon 90 percent of the time (this figure might even be higher), it will become a tossup whether you will win.

Note: A word to the wise. In your backgammon future you will play many games similar to this position where, due to unfortunate rolls, you will be unable to prevent your opponent from establishing a second point on your board. Several moves later you may find yourself in a totally untenable position and when your opponent redoubles, you will hear a strange voice (your own) saying, "I accept." You will be motivated by a feeling of complete frustration at having had a seemingly certain gammon fly out the window. I can assure you that it has happened to me so many times I hate to think about it. By now, I have learned to say "no." I'm still utterly frustrated, but at least I'm better off than being frustrated—plus having the dent in my wallet.

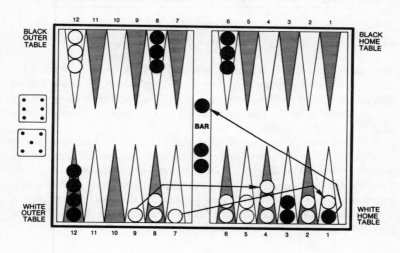

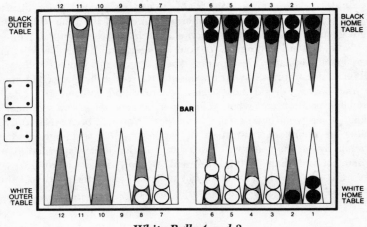

White Rolls 4 and 3
Black owns the cube.

The correct play is to move one man from Black's 11 point to White's bar point. The seemingly obvious play of making White's 2 point, hitting Black's blot, must not be made. You want Black to break his board. By putting his man on the rim, he may roll several times without entering, thus preserving his board.

By not hitting, no matter what Black rolls, with the exception of double 6s or 6 and 1, he will be forced to break that beautiful position in his home board. You should not be concerned about being able to make your 2 point. You should have very little difficulty in doing so. Nor should you worry about Black making your 2 point, for to do so he must give up your 1 point, which will make it that much easier for you to bear off successfully.

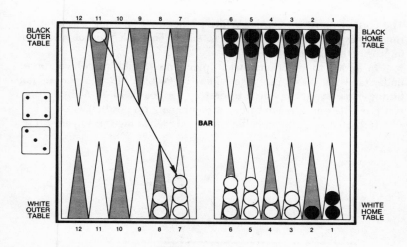

PROBLEM 45-A

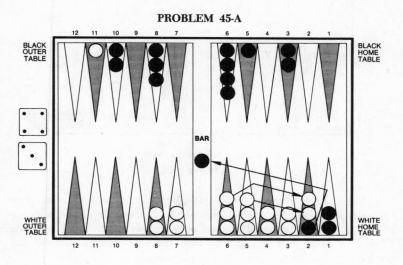

The correct move is to make White's 2 point. By putting Black on the rim, it may take him several rolls to enter. This will prevent him from improving his board.

In order to determine what play one should make, you must understand the play's probable effect. In Problem 45, the play of not hitting causes your opponent to destroy his board. In 45-A, by hitting, you prevent your opponent from strengthening his position.

In both cases "the probable effects" are advantageous to your cause.

● ● ●

PROBLEM 46

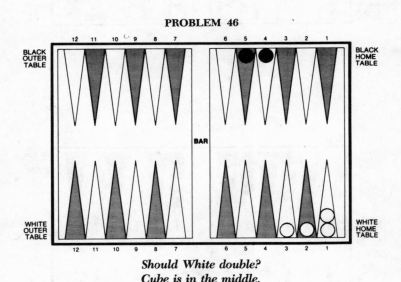

Should White double?
Cube is in the middle.

Yes. White should double. White will automatically bear his men off in two rolls unless he rolls 2 and 1 followed by 2 and 1. Since the odds are 17 to 1 against rolling 2 and 1, to roll it twice consecutively the odds are 17 to 1 × 17 to 1 or 289 to 1 against. We will therefore discard this possibility as totally irrelevant to any calculation.

White can win the game outright with the rolls of double 6s, 5s, 4s, and 3s.

This will occur 4 times out of 36. For the remaining 32 games lets assume White bears off two men. Now, unless Black bears off both men on his roll, White will win. Black will accomplish this only with the rolls of double 6s, 5s, 4s, 3s, 6 and 5, 6 and 4, and 5 and 4 (a total of 10 times out of a possible 36).

If you were to play this same position 36 times, 4 of these times White would end the game in 1 roll. Of the remaining 32 games White will win approximately 23 times, giving White an expected winning total based on probabilities of 27 out of 36 games, or in other words 3 out of every 4 games.

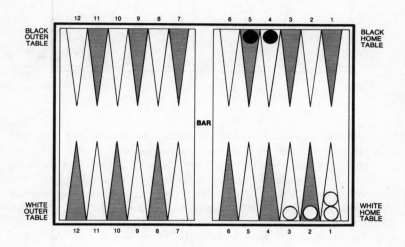

Any time you encounter a position similar to this one—where you must bear off in 2 rolls and where your opponent is not favored to bear off his remaining men in 1 roll if he is to win—you must double. For example, examine 46-A.

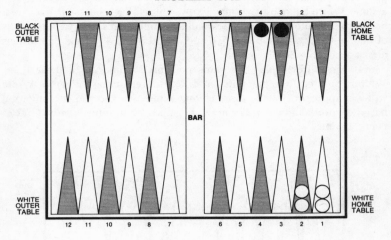

Although you will certainly win fewer times than in the preceding illustration, it will still be more than your opponent.

Out of 36 games you will win 5 times on your first roll (double 6s, 5s, 4s, 3s, and 2s). This leaves 31 games. Of these 31 games, Black will win slightly less than 15 times. (He will fail to bear off both men with any roll that contains a 1 or a 2, with the exception of double 2s. This will occur 19 out of 36 times.)

Therefore, if you were to play this identical game 36 times, you would win slightly more than 21 times (the 5 where you win on the first roll and the 16+ where he fails to bear off both of his men). I'm sure that it is not necessary to say that whenever you will win more than 50 percent of the time you should want to increase the stakes to their maximum.

Now that I have shown you that White must double in the above situation I am going to explain the paradox that exists in backgammon where it is correct for one side to double and yet correct for the other side to accept.

Using the figures from 46-A we came to the conclusion that out of 36 games White would win a little more than 21 times, and Black would win a little less than 15 times. At the end of those 36 games White has doubled Black from 1 to 2.

21 times Black will lose 2 points   − 42
15 times Black will win 2 points   + 30
Black's net   − 12

If Black declined all 36 times, he would have a minus of 36. This is proof positive that Black must accept the double.

●   ●   ●

PROBLEM 47

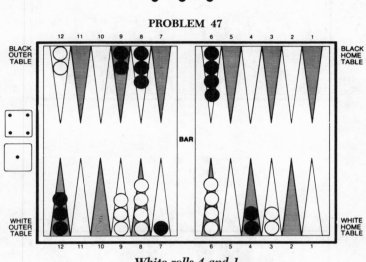

White rolls 4 and 1
Cube is in the middle.

The correct play is to make White's 5 point. You are well ahead in a race, and it appears that your main concern is to be able to bring your men into your home board safely. The 5 point is invaluable in your attempt to do this.

If you were to hit Black's blot on the bar and move this man to your 3 point, you would be giving Black the opportunity to enter on game 1, or 2 points from where he would be a thorn in your side.

You may argue that by not hitting you are giving Black the opportunity to make your bar point. To accomplish this, Black must by necessity then give up your 4 point. If in doing this he leaves a blot on the 4 point, you will have several combinations which will enable you to make your 4 point, or others which will merely hit or hit and pass. This is a play you hope Black makes, for it is to your advantage if he does so.

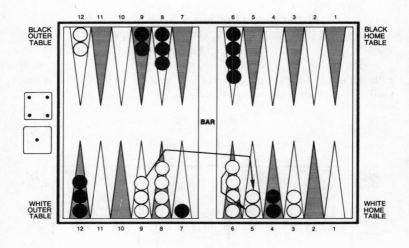

•   •   •

PROBLEM 48

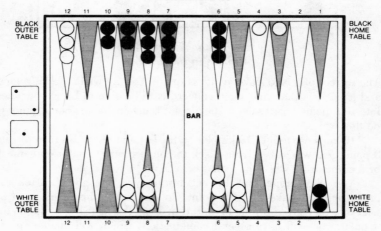

White rolls 2 and 1
Cube is in the middle.

86

The correct play is to make Black's five point. Now that you have established a solid defensive position in Black's home board you may set your sights elsewhere. There no longer is any fear of being pointed on or of being primed. As the game progresses, unless Black is able to escape with his two men which are on your 1 point, he will be forced to move his men past your men on his 5 point. This will ease your escape when it becomes expedient for you to do so.

Your plan now is to make your bar point or 4 point (both if possible), and, in your attempt, it would not be injudicious if you were to leave several blots in your outer board.

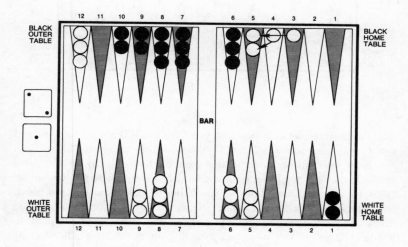

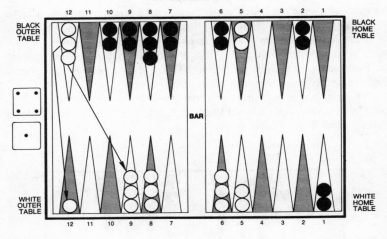

To illustrate, let's assume that you have made Black's five point and that Black's next roll was 5 and 4, with which he made his 2 point.

Now let's further assume that you do not roll any of the good numbers that are available, such as 2 and 1, 6 and 1, 6 and 2, double 2s, 1s, 3s, 6s, etc., that would enable you either to make your bar or 4 point. Instead, your roll is 4 and 1. Your play should be to move one man from Black's 12 point to White's 9 point and one man from Black's 12 point to White's 12 point. You have left 2 blots (you could have left none by moving one man from Black's 12 point to White's 8 point) which increase your chances of making your bar point on your next roll. Black can hit only with the rolls of double 6s, double 3s, or 6 and 5 (the odds are 8 to 1 against this, but these numbers would be good for Black no matter how you elected to play your 4 and 1).

· Let's continue this hypothetical game by having Black roll double 4s. (Admittedly I choose a poor roll for Black. However, one's opponent doesn't always roll good numbers. Also, White's previous roll could have been much better.) Regardless of how Black may decide to play his double 4s, White, on his next turn, should double, for nearly every number will either make White's bar point, 4 point, 3 point, 10 point, or escape with both men from Black's 5 point (depending on how Black's double 4s were played).

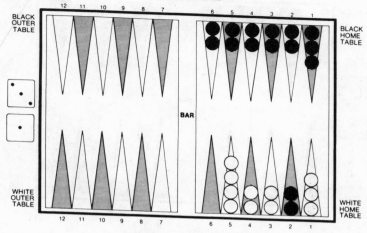

White rolls 3 and 1
Black owns the cube.

The correct play is to move one man from White's 4 point to White's 3 point, and one man from White's 4 point to White's 1 point. On White's next roll, regardless of whether Black leaves one man or two men on White's 2 point, there is no roll that can cause White to leave a blot. On the other hand, had you removed one man from White's 5 point to White's 1 point, the rolls of double 6s, 5s, 4s, 6 and 5, 6 and 4, 6 and 3, 6 and 2, 5 and 4, 5 and 3, 5 and 2, or 4 and 2 would force you to leave a blot (more than 50 percent of the time).

I have given you this rather simple problem in order to make you aware of the possibilities that may exist in other seemingly innocuous situations that may confront you in the future.

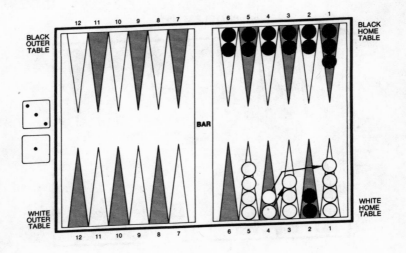

PROBLEM 49-A

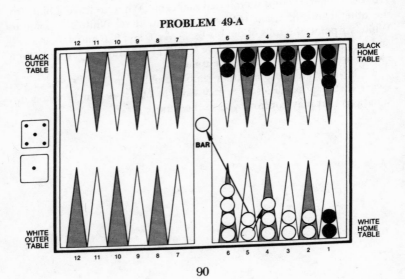

his ne Problem 49-A. If, now, as a result of having seen Problem
to   de the correct move of bearing one man from the 5 point and
ng   e man to White's 4 point, then, in fact, it wasn't such a tough
ve   fter all.
ur
he
on   efully, these two problems have helped train you to recognize
6   lations whenever they may occur. If you are alert, you will think
m   ou move; the result will be that you won't have to say to yourself,
it   d have moved that last 3 and 1 differently."
of
     is brings to mind a favorite quote: "For of all sad words of tongue
6   the saddest are these: 'It might have been!'" That *could* have
r   id as a result of a careless backgammon move.
s

• • •

PROBLEM 50

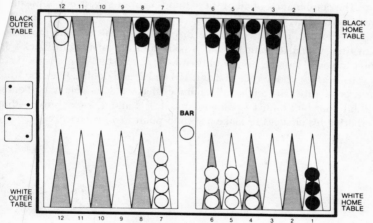

White rolls double 2s
Black owns the cube.

The correct play is to enter on Black's 2 point and move one man in from
White's bar to White's 3 point, and one man from White's 5 point to

White's 3 point. You must avoid hitting Black's blot on his 4 point. [T]additional man can only be detrimental to you, for it will enable Blac[k] make a second point in your board. If you're worried about not be[ing] able to escape from Black's home board, don't be! Now that you h[ave] made your 3 point, only the rolls of double 1s or 6 and 1 can prevent y[our] opponent from being forced to break up his position. Even assuming [the] best possible roll for Black—double 1s—he will still need to roll a 6 [on] his subsequent roll in order to avoid breaking his prime. With the roll [of 6] and 1, which one must assume he would play by moving one man fr[om] White's 1 point to White's 8 point, you would then still be able to [hit] Black's blot on his 4 point, his blot on your 8 point, or make a prime [of] your own.

Eliminating those possibilities (they will happen only 3 out of [36] times) the most probable sequence would be that Black will break his b[ar] or 8 point, close his 4 point, and perhaps be forced to hit your blot on h[is] 2 point. The more Black is forced to hit you, the less he likes it, fo[r] assuming you neither hit any of his blots nor are able to escape, he wi[ll] eventually be forced to open the high points in his board—that is, unles[s] he is lucky enough to roll several 1s followed by 6s, which would free th[e] men on your 1 point.

The combination of all of these things, admittedly, is not impossible[,] but it certainly is very unlikely.

In contrast, if you were to hit Black's blot on his 4 point, move one man from your bar point to your 5 point and one man from Black's 12 point to your 11 point, he would then be able to establish a second point in your board with the rolls of 2 and 1, 3 and 2, and double 1s. Aside from these possibilities, he might roll a number that would enable him to enter and hit your blot on his 4 point—3 and 4 or 2 and 4, for example—thus furthering his chances to make a second point in your board.

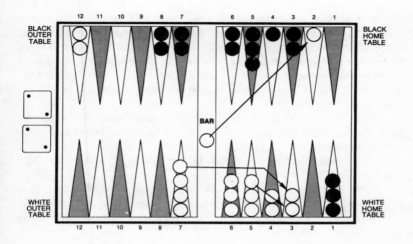

• • •

PROBLEM 51

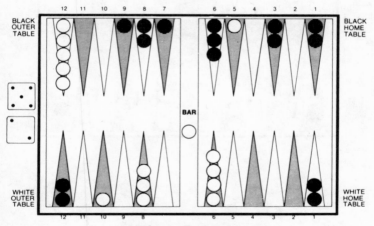

White rolls 5 and 2
White owns the cube.

93

The correct play is to enter on Black's 5 point and move one man from Black's 12 point to White's 11 point. When your opponent has 3 points in his home board and you only have 1, you must be careful about leaving blots. Now that you have an anchor (a sound defensive position in Black's home board) you must attempt to build a board of your own. If your blots on your 10 and 11 points are not hit, you almost surely will be able to make some valuable point.

If you were to hit Black's blot on his bar point, you would surely be re-hit (unless Black rolls double 6s) at least once, and in some cases twice (when Black rolls double 1s, 2s, 3s, or 5s).

The pressure on you would then be not only to enter, but to make a point in Black's board.

Whenever you are under attack and are virtually defenseless (you have no board to threaten with and therefore your opponent has no fear of reëntering), it is a sound policy to establish a point if you are able—any point will do—and keep it!

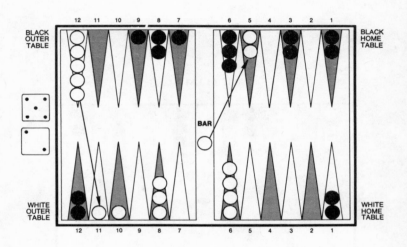

94

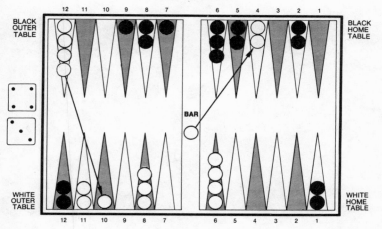

Another example of this strategy is shown in Problem 51-A. Again the proper play is to enter and establish Black's 4 point, and move one man from Black's 12 point to White's 11 point.

As in Problem 51, you must maintain a solid defensive position in Black's home board, which effectively puts a stop to his attack and at the same time starts an offensive of your own. If your blot on this 10 point is not hit, your chances of making a valuable point on your next roll are excellent.

PROBLEM 51-B

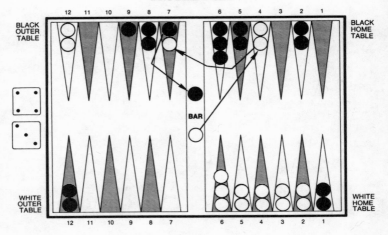

To show a contrast, examine Problem 51-B. Here, Black's position is identical to Problem 51-A. The difference, of course, is the fact that you no longer are "defenseless." Here it is obviously correct to hit Black's blot on his bar point.

• • •

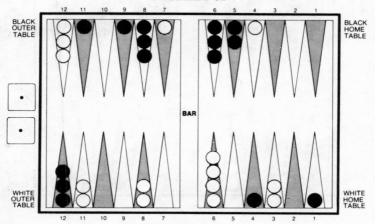

White rolls double 1s
Cube is in the middle.

The correct play is to make White's 4 point, hitting Black's blot. If you were to make your bar point and 5 point, either or both of your two totally exposed men on Black's bar and 4 points would surely be hit. By hitting Black on White's 4 point, several things may occur: (1) Black will fail to enter; this will happen 9 out of 36 times (the rolls of double 3s, 4s, 6s, 6 and 4, 6 and 3, and 4 and 3). If this occurs, White should double because he will expect to hit the additional blots of Black's on Black's 9 and 11 points, or make additional points in his board. (2) Black will enter (but not with double 1s, 2s, or 5s). Since you have forced him to use one of his dice for this purpose, then it is impossible for him to hit either of your blots without having several blots of his own exposed on your subsequent roll. (3) Black will enter with double 1s, 2s, or 5s. These rolls will make the situation very dangerous for you. However, you will still be better off than if you had not made your 4 point.

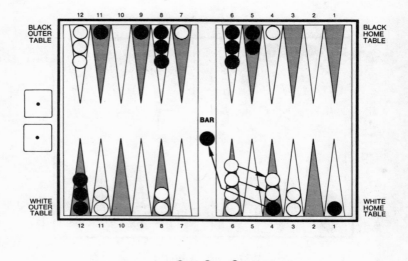

• • •

I'm going to take a break here from the problems to give you a chance to examine the following chart. It delineates the probabilities of entering men from the rim. If you know this already, fine; if not, I feel that this is good information, for it should affect your decision or strategy in many future games of backgammon.

CHANCES OF ENTERING ONE MAN FROM THE BAR

Number of Points Covered By Opponent	Chances (out of 36)	Odds
1	35	35 to 1
2	32	8 to 1
3	27	3 to 1
4	20	5 to 4
5	11	11 to 25

CHANCES OF ENTERING TWO MEN SIMULTANEOUSLY FROM THE BAR

Number of Points Covered By Opponent	Chances (out of 36)	Odds
1	25	25 to 11
2	16	4 to 5
3	9	1 to 3
4	4	1 to 8
5	1	1 to 35

PROBLEM 53

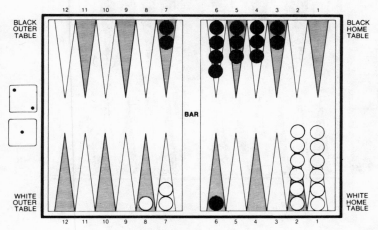

White rolls 2 and 1
Black owns the cube.

The correct play is to move the man from White's 8 point to White's 5 point without hitting Black's blot. If you were to make White's 6 point, you immediately expose your remaining blot on your bar point to being hit with 5 and 2 or 4 and 3.

Failing this, you give Black the opportunity to enter on your 3 point from where you will find it difficult to get your three men past him without leaving a blot. The same will hold true, only slightly less so, if Black enters on your 4 or 5 points.

If he fails to enter at all, several numbers will cause you to leave a blot on your subsequent roll, and some will leave two blots (assuming you had made your 6 point and Black then failed to enter, see what happens when White rolls 6 and 3 or 5 and 3).

Let's find out why it was correct not to make White's 6 point. Although there have been many games like this lost, in a race, you are far less likely to lose the game in this fashion than if you had chosen the other play and then had been forced to leave a blot that was hit. By moving one man to White's 5 point, on your next roll only 6 and 1 or 5 and 1 would cause you to leave a blot. Even assuming this occurs, you still will be a 25 to 11 favorite not to be hit.

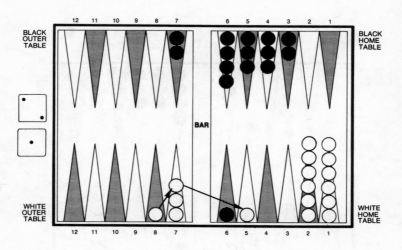

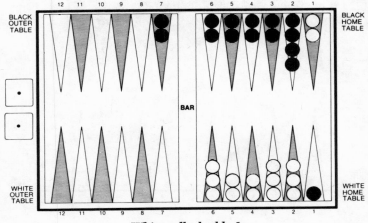

White rolls double 1s
White owns the cube.

The correct play is to move one man from White's 6 point to White's 2 point. Now, unless Black rolls a 6 he will be forced to break his prime. The rolls of double 4s and 3s would be devastating to him. Not only would he be obliged to break his bar point but also some additional point, thus giving you two numbers rather than one with which to escape.

It would have been a poor choice had you closed your board. Eventually, you would have had to open it. Then Black would merely have reëntered and gone on about his business without a care in the world, for by now your board would have been reduced to a shambles. Nor would it have been correct for you to have hit Black's blot, leaving a blot of your own and hoping that Black will roll the 1 without a 6, which would force him to break his prime.

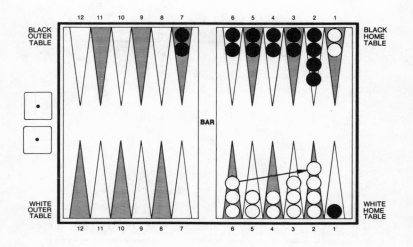

PROBLEM 54-A

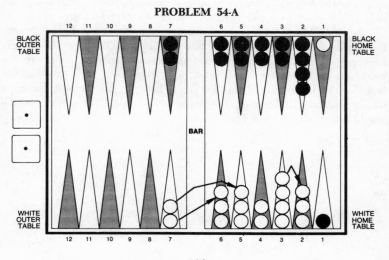

Examine Problem 54-A. Here, although the solution may be more obvious, the principle is identical to the one in Problem 54.

Again, you must not close your board, nor should you hit Black's blot in any fashion whatsoever. If Black is on the bar and cannot move, he will not have to break his prime. The problem, therefore, becomes how best to utilize the play of four aces, so that—assuming Black does not roll a 6 on his next roll—your men will be best placed for your next roll.

• • •

PROBLEM 55

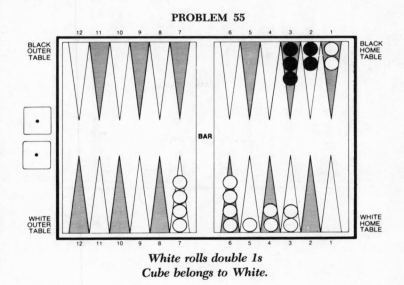

White rolls double 1s
Cube belongs to White.

The correct play is to move one man from White's bar point to White's 5 point and one man from White's 6 point to White's 4 point. The play of bringing four men from your bar point to your 6 point in an attempt to save a gammon is wrong. Unless you hit a blot of Black's it will be most unlikely that you will not be gammoned, for you would need back-to-back large doubles.

103

It appears that Black will be forced to leave a blot on his next roll. (Only the rolls of 2 and 1 or double 2s avoid a blot.) If you are lucky and hit Black's blot (assuming he is forced to leave one), you certainly should save a gammon. You will also have a chance of winning. There is actually a conceivable succession of rolls whereby you could redouble. Let's assume Black rolls 6 and 5 and bears two men from his 3 point. You then roll 2 and something, hitting his blot. Black then rolls 2 and 1. He enters on your 2 point and is forced to split his men on his 2 point, hitting your remaining man, which is on his 1 point. You will now have the opportunity to pick up both of his blots. Even if you hit only one of them, you will have become a favorite to win the game.

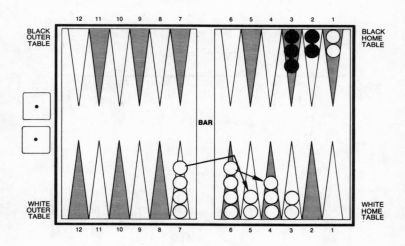

104

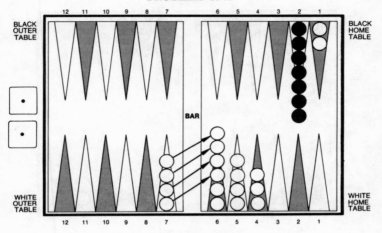

I have presented Problem 55-A to illustrate a direct contrast to Problem 55.

Here, the correct play is to move all four men from White's bar point to White's 6 point. Now, the possibility of saving a gammon is not remote, even without hitting one of Black's men. Nor does it preclude your winning the game. Your plan is to move one man out of Black's board on your next roll, thus forcing him to hit your remaining blot on his 1 point with any roll that contains an ace (with the exception of double 1s). If you hit, once again as in Problem 55, you should be able to save a gammon and give yourself a small chance of winning.

• • •

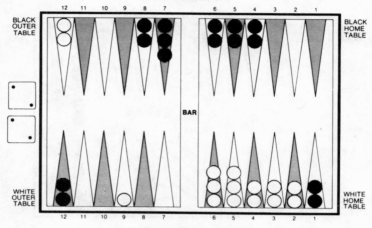

White rolls double 2s
Black owns the cube.

The correct play is to move both men from Black's 12 point to White's 9 point. This position is an example of when a prime is a liability rather than an asset. To make the bar point you would also be forced to leave a blot on Black's 12 point. You can ill afford to be hit with Black's position, as strong as it is.

For example, let's assume you have made the prime, leaving your blot on Black's 12 point, and Black then rolls a 1 and something, hitting your blot. You then roll 2 and 5—(or 1 and 5 or 3 and 5). You enter on Black's 2 point and are forced to break that prime you so carefully made. Not only have you broken it, but you have been forced to leave an exposed man. Even if he is not hit, you will find that your board will rapidly deteriorate unless you are able to escape from Black's board. This assumes your blot is hit. Now assume it isn't hit. You may now encounter difficulties in clearing your bar point preparatory to bearing off. One of the criteria you should use when determining whether you should make primes in positions similar to this, is whether you are trying to block your opponent's escape or whether you would prefer that he did. Obviously there is little chance that you'll lose this game in a race. You could lose, however, if, in bearing off, you exposed a blot which was hit.

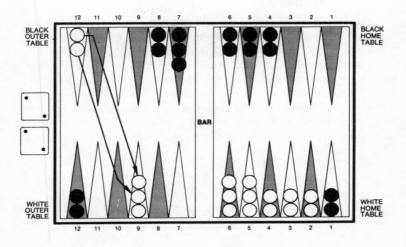

PROBLEM 56-A

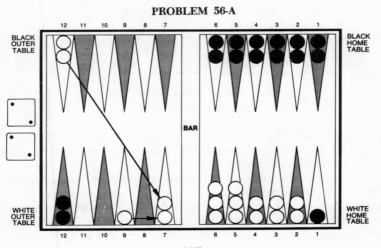

107

Once again to illustrate a direct contrast, examine Problem 56-A.

Now it behooves you to make the prime, preventing Black's escape. Nor are you concerned about being hit on Black's 12 point. If Black hits you, you will merely wait until he is forced to open his board, whereupon you will resume your plan of closing your board and then bearing off.

One final thought concerning Problem 56: If you are forced to leave a blot on your 9 point (having used the play of moving both men from Black's 12 point to White's 9 point), which would occur if your subsequent roll were 6 and 5, this blot could only be hit with 6 and 2, a 17 to 1 chance.

● ● ●

PROBLEM 57

White rolls 4 and 1
Black owns the cube.

The four is easy—the one is difficult. It may seemingly be unimportant where the ace is taken; the only correct move, however, is to move from Black's 4 point to Black's 5 point.

The reason for this move is that the only number that you have to fear that Black can roll is double 5s. If you move any other 1 in Black's outer board or your outer board, with the roll of double 5s, Black will enter and move to his 5 point. Thus, you will have just a 1 with which to hit this blot with your man on his 4 point. If you are on his 5 point, he will be forced to hit you. You will therefore be on the rim and will have a chance to hit Black's blot on his 2 point, plus his newly arrived blot on his 5 point. You have increased your chances of hitting from 11 out of 36 to 22 out of 36, exactly double.

If Black rolls 5 and 6, 5 and 3, or 5 and 2, you will have three men directly bearing on his resulting blot. If Black's roll is 5 and 4, hitting your blot on your 9 point, you will have the opportunity to hit his blot on his 2 point, plus re-hitting his blot now on your 9 point. If Black rolls 5 and 1 (his best roll), he will save his blot on his 2 point. You're still okay, however, for you will be able to hit his blot on your 5 point with 4s, 7s, 8s, 12s, and 15s.

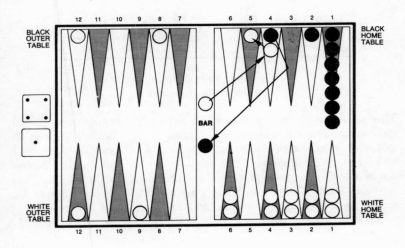

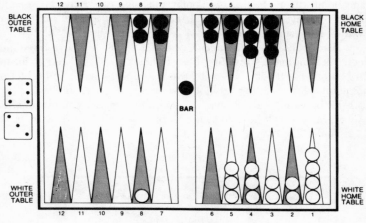

White rolls 6 and 3
Black owns the cube.

This is a relatively easy problem, yet one which is quite often played incorrectly. The correct play is to move 3 from White's 8 point to White's 5 point and then bear the same man off. If Black does not enter on his turn, you will expose a blot only with the roll of 6 and 5 (2 chances out of 36)—if you move a 6 from White's 8 point to White's 2 point, and a 3 from White's 5 point to White's 2 point. The rolls of double 6s, 5s, and 4s would cause you to leave a blot (3 chances out of 36—or, in other words a 50 percent increase).

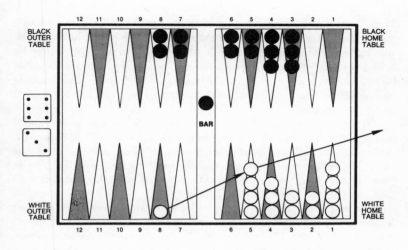

•   •   •

PROBLEM 59

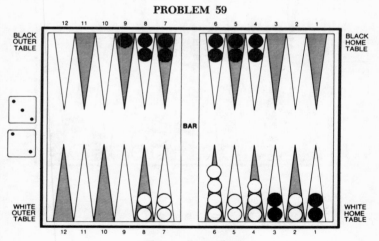

White rolls 3 and 2
Black owns the cube.

111

The correct play is to move both men from your bar point to your 5 and 4 points. If Black maintains his position in your board (which he should be able to do since he has five men in his outer board to play with before he is forced to move any of the men in your board), you will be forced to leave a blot with the rolls of 6 and 5, 6 and 1, and 5 and 1. The resulting blot on your 8 point will be exposed to being hit with any 5, 4 and 1, or 6 and 1 (15 chances).

If you were to move both men from your 8 point to your 6 and 5 points, you will be forced to leave a blot with the rolls of 6 and 5, 5 and 4, double 5s, and 3s (the same number of chances of exposure as in the first play). The difference, however, is that the resulting blot, whether it be on your bar or 5 point, will be exposed to 20 chances of being hit versus 15 chances with the correct play.

An additional factor which must be taken into consideration is that by moving your two men on your bar, your two men on your 8 point will move in safely with 17 combinations. If you have two men on your bar, these men will move in safely with only 14 combinations.

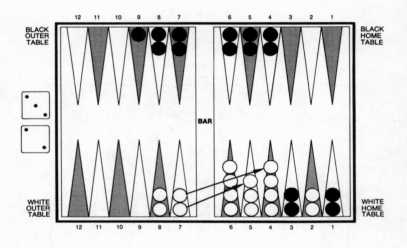

112

PROBLEM 60

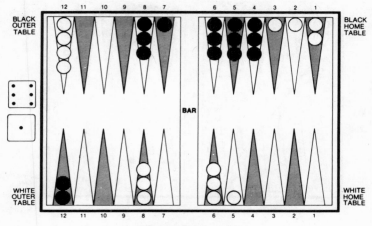

White rolls 6 and 1
White owns the cube.

The correct play is to make Black's 3 point and move one man from Black's 12 point to White's bar point. You now have the necessary elements for a back game. You have established two good points in Black's board, and you are far behind in a race. Unless you roll extremely large numbers on your next several rolls, you should, by the time Black starts to bear his men off, have a good position on your side of the board (your 3, 4, 5, 6, and bar points or close to it). Therefore, if and when Black leaves a blot which you hit, he will find entry and escape very difficult.

An attempt to win this game by any other means except a back game will be doomed to failure unless you perform miracles and your opponent plays poorly.

The temptation to hit Black's blot on Black's bar point, and make your 5 point, must be resisted. This play would leave you with no points in Black's board and four blots which could prove to be disastrous.

113

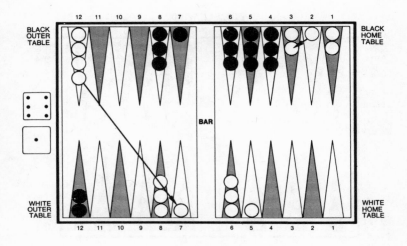

• • •

PROBLEM 61

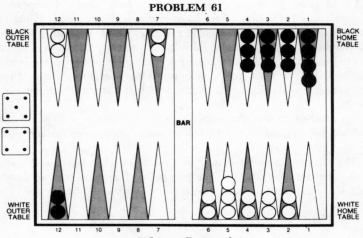

White rolls 5 and 4
White owns the cube.

The correct play is to make White's 1 point. You don't like to give up your 6 point, but unfortunately you must do so. You still have a 5 point board, which should be sufficient to win with in the event you hit one of Black's blots (you still may be able to hit and remake your 6 point). It appears that Black may have to break on his next roll. Any combination with a 4, 5, or 6—except double 4s, 5s, or 6s, and 6 and 1—will leave a blot. Some rolls, such as 4 and 1, 5 and 1, and 4 and 2, will force Black to expose two men. If you were to have moved your men on Black's 12 point to your 8 and 9 points, then, when and if Black left a blot on your 12 point, you would have only 6s (or combinations of 6s) to hit with. With the correct play, you greatly increase your chances of hitting. You also (and you should consider this only a fringe benefit, not a determining factor) prevent him from playing double 1s to his advantage.

A quick example of the added rewards of maintaining Black's 12 point would be in the event of Black's rolling 6 and 2, 6 and 3, 6 and 4, or 6 and 5. The man which he will be forced to leave on your 12 point will be exposed to 24 chances out of 36 to be hit. If you did not have Black's 12 point, you would have only 17 chances to hit. In effect, therefore, you would go from a 2 to 1 favorite to hit to a slight underdog. The same holds true (with slight variations) with other rolls, such as 5 and 2, 5 and 3, 5 and 4, etc.

As for a possible alternate play—for instance, leaving one man on Black's 12 point instead of breaking your 6 point—you would expose yourself to being hit with an ace. If this occurs, no matter where Black leaves his men, you would no longer be favored to hit. You may fail to enter, and that may be all that your opponent will need to clear his two men.

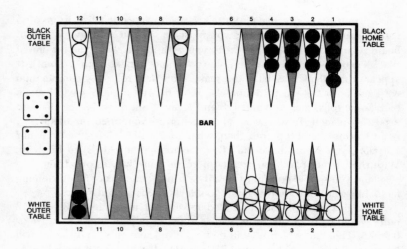

• • •

PROBLEM 62

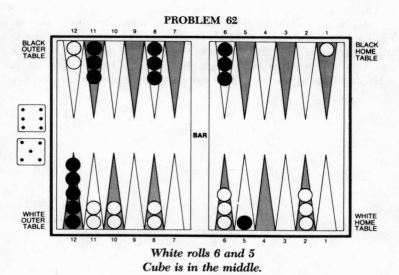

White rolls 6 and 5
Cube is in the middle.

The correct play is to move one man from Black's 1 point to Black's 12 point. You disdain hitting Black's blot on your 5 point for the reason that you are so far ahead in the race that you plan to double on your next roll. Now that you have no problems other than getting your men into your home board without being hit, Black can hardly accept. If he does, all the better for you.

If you choose to make your 5 point, you are immediately exposed to being hit by a 4 and 6. Admittedly it's only a 17 to 1 risk, but why risk it at all, when to all intents and purposes you have won the game with the other play. Even if Black doesn't roll 6 and 4, he may roll double 1s or 3s, which will improve his position. You may then find it more difficult to escape with your lone man on Black's 1 point.

This problem will show you that when you have a choice of moves you should determine which offers you the best chances of winning or the least of losing, then select that one.

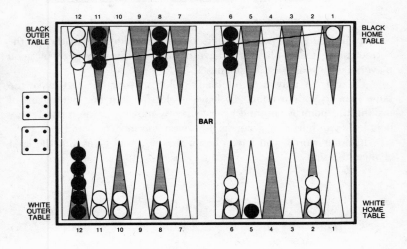

117

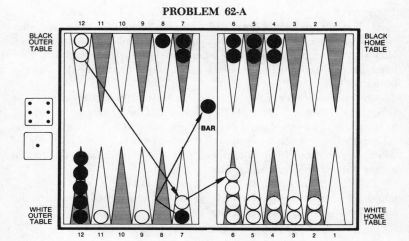

To illustrate this point further, look at Problem 62-A: Although the correct move seems obvious, I have often seen this game lost by good players because of poor judgment.

The correct play is to hit Black's blot on your bar and move the same man to your 6 point. To leave a blot on your bar with plans of making this point is an unnecessary risk. By moving to the 6 point, only double 1s can hurt you, whereas otherwise you include 1 and 6.

In other words, you have chosen the play that gives you the least chance of losing.

● ● ●

PROBLEM 63

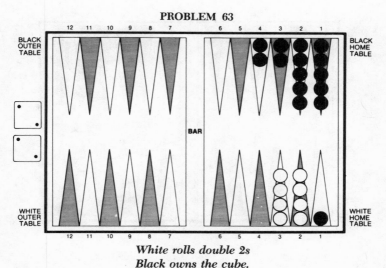

White rolls double 2s
Black owns the cube.

The correct play is to bear four men off your 2 point.

The totally safe play of making your 1 point and bearing two men from the 2 point is inferior. It is almost inconceivable that you could lose this game. Therefore, the only important thing is to make the play that will give you the best chance to win a gammon or a backgammon. By bearing four men off, any roll of Black's that does not enable him to get out of your board will give you the opportunity to roll double 3s, 4s, 5s, or 6s—which would win a backgammon for you. With the play of hitting and bearing two men off, you practically eliminate any chance of winning a backgammon, for at best it will take you 2 rolls to bear off your remaining six men.

As for winning a gammon, the same applies. Your chances of bearing four men from your 3 point in 2 rolls is greater than that of bearing six men off from the 1, 2, and 3 points. It is true that you will gain something with the play of hitting when your opponent fails to enter. In that case, however, it means that he is rolling small numbers, and you will win the gammon in any event. Even if Black rolls double 5s, you still could win a gammon had you borne off four men. With the other move, this would be impossible.

119

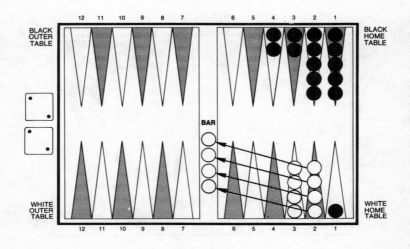

• • •

PROBLEM 64

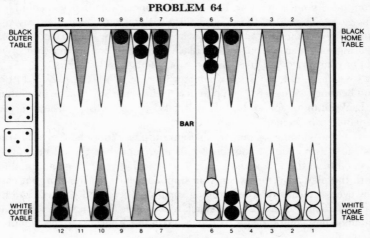

White rolls 6 and 5
Black owns the cube.

The correct play is to move one man from Black's 12 point to White's bar point, and one man from Black's 12 point to White's 8 point. If your blot on White's 8 point is not hit (11 chances out of 36), you would have to be very unfortunate to leave any more blots in your attempt to enter your men into your home board.

If you were to play safe by moving both men from your bar to your 2 and 1 points, your two men on Black's 12 point would find it exceedingly difficult to get to safety. Only the rolls of double 5s or 6s would clear these men without leaving a blot. Double 3s and 1s can't be played; double 4s would leave a blot on your 6 point; and even with double 2s—assuming you moved to your 9 point—you would still need a marvelous roll to get these men past Black's block on your 5 point.

Simply stated, by avoiding a blot on this roll, your position will most likely be a lot worse 1 or 2 rolls later.

If, for example, you had moved both men from your bar point, and your next roll was 6 and anything except another 6, see how you would have increased the probabilities of your being hit. Add to that the fact that Black surely would have made his board a lot more dangerous with his previous roll. Even if you were able to delay this horrible situation by rolling some numbers which would allow you to play in your inner board, eventually (unless you rolled double 5s or 6s) you would be forced into it.

The added benefits of leaving the blot on your 8 point if Black does hit are (1) he may not cover his blot on his 5 point, and (2) he may be forced to leave a blot on your 5 point, which you could hit.

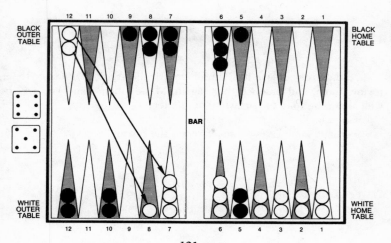

121

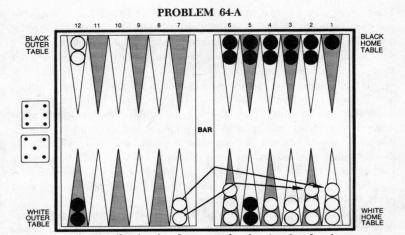

Examine Problem 64-A. The correct play now is to move both men from your bar point to your 2 and 1 points. Although *your* position is identical to that in Problem 64, the overall position is vastly different. Since Black must break either his board, his block on your 12 point, or your 5 point on his next roll, it would be poor judgment to expose a man unnecessarily. Delay in this position should be advantageous to you.

● ● ●

And there you have it—64 problems, with variations. Practice them, review them, and practice them again. Master them—and you will be well along the road to backgammon mastery.

Good luck!

Perhaps someday we'll meet across the board.